Preparing for the ACSM
HEALTH/FITNESS INSTRUCTOR
Certification Examination

Larry D. Isaacs, PhD
and
Roberta Pohlman, PhD

Wright State University
Dayton, Ohio

Human Kinetics

To my children, Brooke and Timothy; to the memory of my loving parents, Linwood and Gracie; and to the memory of a best friend, Burt
—Larry D. Isaacs
To my friends and family for their love and support —Roberta Pohlman

Library of Congress Cataloging-in-Publication Data

Isaacs, Larry D. (Larry David), 1949-
  Preparing for the ACSM health/fitness instructor certification examination / Larry D. Isaacs, Roberta Pohlman.
    p. cm.
  Includes bibliographical references (p.).
  ISBN 0-87322-732-8
    1. Personal trainers--Certification--United States--Examinations--Study guides.   I. Pohlman, Roberta, 1951-   . II. Title.
  GV428.7.I73   1997
  613.7'11'076--dc21   97-21454
                                                              CIP

ISBN: 0-87322-732-8

Copyright © 1998 by Larry D. Isaacs and Roberta Pohlman

This preparatory text was not produced by ACSM. The American College of Sports Medicine, ACSM, ACSM Health/Fitness Director, ACSM Health/Fitness Instructor, ACSM Exercise Leader, ACSM Program Director, ACSM Exercise Specialist, and ACSM Exercise Test Technologist are all trademarks of the American College of Sports Medicine, Inc.

Acquisitions Editor: Scott Wikgren; **Developmental Editor:** Andrew Smith; **Assistant Editors:** Tony Callihan, John Wentworth, and Sandra Merz Bott; **Editorial Assistant:** Jennifer Hemphill; **Copyeditor:** Joyce Sexton; **Proofreader:** Sue Fetters; **Graphic Designer:** Stuart Cartwright; **Graphic Artist:** Sandra Meier; **Photo Editor:** Boyd LaFoon; **Cover Designer:** Robert Reuther; **Printer:** Versa Press

Printed in the United States of America   10   9   8   7   6   5   4   3   2   1

Human Kinetics
Web site: http://www.humankinetics.com/

United States: Human Kinetics, P.O. Box 5076, Champaign, IL 61825-5076, 1-800-747-4457
e-mail: humank@hkusa.com

Canada: Human Kinetics, Box 24040, Windsor, ON N8Y 4Y9, 1-800-465-7301 (in Canada only)
e-mail: humank@hkcanada.com

Europe: Human Kinetics, P.O. Box IW14, Leeds LS16 6TR, United Kingdom, (44) 1132 781708
e-mail: humank@hkeurope.com

Australia: Human Kinetics, 57A Price Avenue, Lower Mitcham, South Australia 5062, (08) 277 1555
e-mail: humank@hkaustralia.com

New Zealand: Human Kinetics, P.O. Box 105-231, Auckland 1, (09) 523 3462
e-mail: humank@hknewz.com

CONTENTS

PREFACE

Preparing for the ACSM Health/Fitness Instructor Certification Examination is the only comprehensive preparatory text of its kind written specifically for the purpose of preparing you to pass this highly sought-after certification offered through the prestigious American College of Sports Medicine (ACSM). In fact, ACSM certifications are considered the "gold standard" among exercise science professionals.

To help you get the most from this preparatory text, we have divided it into three parts. In part I, we carefully walk you through the certification process (chapter 1). Here you will learn about the eligibility criteria for certification, about registration procedures for the certification examination, and about the general structure of both the written and practical portions of the certification process. Perhaps most important, we then provide detailed information about both the written (chapter 2) and the practical (chapter 3) examinations. Here we describe the 10 content areas that the written certification examination covers and even tell you approximately how many questions you can expect in each area. In addition, we highlight test-taking suggestions and special test-taking precautions that will undoubtedly improve your test score by reducing your chance of making an unnecessary error. We then describe, in detail, the four aspects of the practical examination (chapter 3). Not only will you learn the specific tasks that you will likely be required to perform at each of the four practical examination stations, but you will also have a list of preparatory strategies specifically geared to this aspect of the certification examination, including tips on how to get the practical experience necessary to pass this part of the ACSM Health/Fitness Instructor examination.

In part II you will find nearly 600 practice study questions. More specifically, for each of the 10 examination content areas there is an entire chapter of study questions. These study questions are similar to the questions you are likely to encounter on your written certification examination. And perhaps most important, each practice study question is designed to assess your knowledge, skills, and abilities (KSAs) as used by ACSM to describe the minimal competencies necessary to obtain ACSM certification. Each chapter of study questions ends with a detailed answer sheet. On the answer sheet you will find the answer to each study question, and in addition a reference to a source, with page number, where you can find more information about the concept. Furthermore, the specific ACSM KSA being measured by each question is identified. This arrangement not only will save you time in referring you to important study materials, but also will allow you to pinpoint specific areas of weakness within each of the 10 examination (KSA) categories. Part II ends with two special chapters, each addressing a special form of questioning to which you will need to respond during the certification process. More specifically, in chapter 14 you will learn how to solve metabolic equations, and in chapter 15 you will learn how to answer questions when information is presented in the form of a case study. These chapters will help prepare you for questions posed during both the written and the practical portions of the examination.

The third and final part of this preparatory text takes the form of appendixes. Appendix A is a complete practice Health/Fitness Instructor certification examination containing 103 questions. This practice certification examination was designed to simulate the actual written examination in terms of length, time limit (three hours), and question emphasis (i.e., number of questions from each KSA examination category). When taking this practice examination, be sure to record your answers on the blank score sheet provided in appendix B. This preparatory text ends with a specially designed answer sheet (appendix C) for the practice examination and a practice examination profile sheet (appendix D). The first part of this answer sheet simply provides a list of answers (#1-103) for the practice examination. However, on the second portion of the answer sheet, the answers are classified according to the 10 KSA categories. This special breakdown will allow you to fill in the profile sheet in order to identify specific areas of strength and weakness. Obviously you will want to devote additional study time to identified areas of weakness before attempting ACSM certification.

In summary, this preparatory text, *Preparing for the ACSM Health/ Fitness Instructor Certification Examination,* will help you develop your confidence in test-taking strategies for successfully obtaining ACSM certification.

ABBREVIATIONS

ADP	andenosine diphosphate
ATP	adenosine triphosphate
AV	atrioventricular
a-$\dot{V}O_2$ diff	arteriovenous oxygen difference
BMI	body mass index
BP	blood pressure
Ca^{++}	calcium
CAD	coronary artery disease
CHO	carbohydrate
CP	creatine phosphate
CPR	cardiopulmonary resuscitation
CRF	cardiorespiratory function
DBP	diastolic blood pressure
DOMS	delayed onset of muscle soreness
ECG	electrocardiogram
EMS	emergency medical system
FIT	frequency, intensity, time
GXT	graded exercise test
HDL-C	high-density lipoprotein-cholesterol
HR	heart rate
HRR	heart rate reserve
IDDM	insulin-dependent diabetes mellitus
kcal	kilocalories
LDL-C	low-density lipoprotein-cholesterol
MET	metabolic equivalent
mm Hg	millimeters of mercury
MVC	maximal voluntary contraction
O_2	oxygen
OBLA	onset of blood lactate accumulation
PC	phosphocreatine
PVC	preventricular contraction
PWC	physical work capacity
Q	cardiac output
RM	repetition maximum
ROM	range of motion
RPE	rate of perceived exertion
SA	sinoatrial node
SBP	systolic blood pressure
SV	stroke volume
TC	total cholesterol
USDA	United States Department of Agriculture
VLDL-C	very low density lipoprotein-cholesterol
$V_E/\dot{V}O_2$	ventilatory equivalent
$\dot{V}O_2$max	maximal oxygen consumption

PART
1

ABOUT THE EXAMINATION

CHAPTER 1

Understanding and Preparing for ACSM Certification

© W. Lynn Seldon

Congratulations! You have chosen to become certified by an organization considered to be the "gold standard" among professionals in the fields of health, fitness, and cardiac rehabilitation. The American College of Sports Medicine (ACSM) certification tracks, as you will read, are designed to increase your competency in your specific area of interest. When you receive your ACSM certification, you will know that you are among an elite group of professionals internationally recognized for their knowledge, skills, and abilities in the fields of health and fitness. Now let's begin by examining the ACSM certification process.

ACSM CERTIFICATION

Certification through ACSM is organized around two distinct tracks, each comprised of three levels. The Health/Fitness Track, the primary emphasis in this text, consists of certifications (Exercise Leader, Health/Fitness Instructor, Health/Fitness Director) that are geared toward individuals who wish to provide program leadership to apparently healthy individuals and, in some cases, individuals with controlled disease. These programs are primarily preventive in nature. In contrast, certifications within the Clinical Track (Exercise Test Technologist, Exercise Specialist, Program Director) involve working both with individuals at high risk of disease and with individuals who have known diseases (ACSM, 1995).

In this text we will focus exclusively on the second level of certification within the Health/Fitness Track, namely, that of Health/Fitness Instructor. It is important to note that certification at an advanced level requires the candidate to possess the knowledge base and skills associated with that level of certification as well as the knowledge base and skills required of any level below that level of certification. Therefore, certification at the level of Health/Fitness Instructor requires the candidate to demonstrate a command of the knowledge base and skills at both the level of Exercise Leader and the level of Health/Fitness Instructor.

ELIGIBILITY CRITERIA FOR
HEALTH/FITNESS INSTRUCTOR CERTIFICATION

Documentation of formal educational training (degrees) and/or work-related experience is *not required* for certification at the Health/

Fitness Instructor level. The only certifiable documentation required for taking the certification examination is a current validation in CPR. Nevertheless, the ACSM Certification Subcommittee (ACSM, 1995) has strongly recommended that the potential certification candidate have

1. formal training comparable to an undergraduate degree in a health, fitness, or closely related field of study and

2. practical knowledge and work-related experience in the area of exercise leadership as well as counseling skills in the areas of lifestyle behavior modification, risk factor and health status identification, fitness appraisal, and exercise prescription. Chapter 3 explains in greater detail the depth of work-related experience recommended as preparation for certification.

OBTAINING AN APPLICATION

Regardless of your time frame for obtaining certification, we recommend that you request an application as soon as possible. You can obtain an application by contacting the ACSM Certification Resource Center at 800-486-5643. Ask for the current ACSM Certification Resource Catalog. This catalog will contain an application, a list of dates and locations of planned certification sites, and a list of recommended publications for study.

REGISTERING FOR THE CERTIFICATION EXAMINATION

When completing the Health/Fitness Instructor application, you will note that you need to make several decisions. More specifically, you will need to select a preferred certification site and date as well as an alternative in case your first choice is not available. While ACSM requires that your application be postmarked 30 days prior to the examination, we suggest that to improve your chances of gaining admission to your preferred site you submit the application as soon as possible. Also note that many of the certification sites offer a precertification workshop (see discussion later in this chapter). If you plan to attend the workshop before the certification examination, you must note this on the application. You will also be required to sign a statement verifying current CPR certification.

After completing the application, you should make two photocopies. Keep one photocopy for your records and mail the original, along with one photocopy and the appropriate fees (check, money order, MasterCard or VISA), to the address listed at the bottom of the application. Please note that this address is that of the ACSM National Center in Indianapolis, Indiana, *not* that of the ACSM Resource Center from which you obtained the application.

TEST STRUCTURE AND ADMINISTRATION

The ACSM Health/Fitness Instructor certification examination has two components: a written examination consisting of approximately 100 multiple-choice questions and a 60-minute practical examination. Each of these certification components is designed to test the knowledge, skills, and abilities (KSAs, formerly referred to by ACSM as general and specific learning objectives) that a certified Health/Fitness Instructor needs in order to perform his or her duties. These KSAs are organized around the 10 categories outlined in table 1.1 (see also ACSM, 1995, pp. 307-330).

The practical examination will also require you to demonstrate knowledge and skill in performing such tasks as identifying and collecting anthropometric data, including skinfolds and circumferential assessments; demonstrating flexibility and strength exercises; administering tests of flexibility and muscular endurance; and preparing to administer, as well as administering, selected aspects of a physical work capacity (PWC) test. In both chapter 2, "The Written

Table 1.1   The 10 ACSM KSA Categories
Functional Anatomy and Biomechanics
Exercise Physiology
Human Development and Aging
Pathophysiology and Risk Factors
Human Behavior and Psychology
Health Appraisal and Fitness Testing
Emergency Procedures and Safety
Exercise Programming
Nutrition and Weight Management
Program Administration and Management

Examination," and chapter 3, "The Practical Examination," we explain the details of each of these examinations and offer practical advice on how to prepare for each.

WHAT TO EXPECT ON TEST DAY

Knowing what to expect on test day can greatly reduce test anxiety. Note the following points about the test-day procedures you will be required to follow:

✓ Arrive at the predetermined certification site at least 15 minutes before the time the test is scheduled to begin. This holds true for both the written and the practical examinations.

✓ Upon checking in, you will be required to show proof of positive identification by producing a driver's license or passport. Anyone unable to provide one of these forms of identification *will not* be allowed to take the certification examination.

✓ Bring several number 2 pencils and a calculator to the written examination. The calculator must be of the simplest variety; *no programmable calculators* are allowed.

✓ At the designated examination time, the written certification examination will be distributed to each candidate. The examination will be in an individually sealed envelope. You are *not* to open the envelope until instructed to do so. From the time this instruction is given you will be allowed no more than three hours to complete the written examination.

✓ When turning in the completed examination, you will be required to place the test questions, as well as your score sheet, back into the envelope. The envelope will be sealed and a special label will be placed across the envelope's sealed tab. To complete the process you will be asked to place your signature onto this special label.

✓ With regard to the practical examination, a special briefing session is typically scheduled the day before the examination. At this time you will be given an explanation of the exam process and a schedule confirming the time of your examination. You will also have the opportunity to familiarize yourself with the equipment that will be utilized during the practical examination. This is especially helpful for candidates who have not participated in the precertification workshop.

SCORING

Both the written and the practical examinations are scored at the ACSM National Office. A passing score for the written examination is determined by the ACSM Certification Subcommittee on the basis of normative data. The minimal score for passing is (at this time) 67 percent (ACSM, 1994).

Even though the practical examination is evaluated on the basis of your performance at each of four examination stations (see chapter 3), your score will be calculated as a function of your overall performance. While questions on the practical examination are differentially weighted, you cannot fail this portion of the certification process by missing any one question. Once again, the score needed to pass the practical examination is determined annually by the ACSM Certification Subcommittee (ACSM, 1996).

NOTIFICATION OF RESULTS

Within four to six weeks you will receive your test results by mail for both the written and the practical examinations. Results of both the written and practical examinations are reported as Pass/Fail. However, candidates who fail the practical examination will receive a detailed analysis based on KSAs associated with selected questions from the practical examination. The purpose of this analysis is to give you information regarding personal strengths and weaknesses identified during the practical examination. To receive certification, you must obtain a passing score on both the written and the practical examinations.

RETESTING PROCEDURES

If you fail either the written or the practical examination, you will be required to take a retest on the component you did not pass. All the registration procedures described earlier hold true for the retest as well. While there is no mandatory waiting period before one can attempt to pass a retest, we *strongly recommend* that you use the information presented on the notification of results to prepare for retesting. You must, however, complete retesting prior to December 31 of the year after the certification date. If you do not meet this requirement, you will need to begin the certification process over again.

PREPARING FOR CERTIFICATION

Preparation is the key to successfully passing the Health/Fitness Instructor certification examination. In this section we offer several suggestions regarding ways in which you can prepare effectively.

PRECERTIFICATION WORKSHOPS

As we have already mentioned, three- to four-day precertification workshops are offered at many of the certification examination sites. These workshops consist of approximately 20 hours of lecture covering all of the vital KSA categories. In addition, at a workshop you will have ample time to practice the tasks you will need to perform during the practical examination. More specifically, practicum sessions include submaximal testing; body composition, muscular strength, and endurance testing; and an opportunity to work with case studies. We highly recommend this preparatory experience.

ACSM HEALTH/FITNESS INSTRUCTOR CERTIFICATION STUDY PACKET

You can order a specially prepared 18-page study packet through the ACSM Resource Center (phone 800-486-5643; fax 800-447-8438). This packet contains a brief diagnostic examination consisting of only 10 multiple-choice questions, an explanation of the written and practical examinations, and most important, a number of tables containing information that is essential for you to put to memory in order to pass both the written and the practical examinations. All but one of these tables now appear in the fifth edition of *ACSM's Guidelines for Exercise Testing and Prescription* (ACSM, 1995). The remaining table (ACSM Cycle Ergometry Protocol) can be found in a number of publications, including the work of Howley and Franks (1992). For your convenience, table 1.2 identifies each of these important tables (as well as a couple of additional important tables) and tells you where you can find them. We suggest that you photocopy each of these tables for easy access, since you will be referring to them throughout your course of study.

Table 1.2 Important Tables to Study		
Tables to study	Source*	Page number
Coronary Artery Disease Risk Factors	1	18
ACSM Recommendations for Medical Exam and Exercise Testing Prior to Participation and Physician Supervision of Exercise Tests	1	25
Informed Consent (Sample Form)	1	43-44
Standardized Description of Skinfold Sites and Procedures	1	56
Standardized Description of Circumferential Sites and Procedures	1	58
Rating of Perceived Exertion Scales	1	68
YMCA Cycle Ergometry Protocol	1	69
General Procedures for Submaximal Testing of Cardiorespiratory Endurance Using a Cycle Ergometer	1	70
Push-up Test Procedures	1	82
Trunk Flexion Test Procedures	1	83
Absolute and Relative Indications for Termination of an Exercise Test	1	97
ACSM Cycle Ergometry Protocol	2	174

*1. ACSM. (1995). *ACSM's guidelines for exercise testing and prescription* (5th ed.). Baltimore: Williams and Wilkins.

2. Howley, E.T. & Franks, B.D. (1992). *Health fitness instructor's handbook* (2nd ed.). Champaign, IL: Human Kinetics.

SUGGESTIONS FOR USING THIS PREPARATORY TEXT

Now that you have a better understanding of the certification process, you should be ready and eager to begin preparing. Here we list a few suggestions on how you can best use this text as you begin the preparatory process.

- Obtain copies of the printed materials that are most critical for study. In addition to this text, we suggest the sources listed in table 1.3.

Table 1.3 Key Sources of Information*
ACSM. (1993). *ACSM's resource manual for guidelines for exercise testing and prescription* (2nd ed.). Malvern, PA: Lea and Febiger.
ACSM. (1995). *ACSM's guidelines for exercise testing and prescription* (5th ed.). Baltimore: Williams and Wilkins.
Baechle, T.R. (Ed.). (1994). *Essentials of strength training and conditioning*. Champaign, IL: Human Kinetics.
Heyward, V.H. (1991). *Advanced fitness assessment and exercise prescription* (2nd ed.). Champaign, IL: Human Kinetics.
Howley, E.T., and Franks, B.D. (1997). *Health fitness instructor's handbook* (3rd ed.). Champaign, IL: Human Kinetics.

*You should also obtain a basic anatomy and exercise physiology textbook.

- Begin by reviewing the ACSM KSAs on pages 307-330 in the fifth edition of *ACSM's Guidelines for Exercise Testing and Prescription* (ACSM, 1995). These numbered KSAs describe in detail the competencies you will be required to exhibit in order to receive your Health/Fitness Instructor certification. Then, note that as you work through this book you will find an answer key at the end of each study-question chapter (chapters 4-13) specific to a KSA. This key contains the answer to each study question, a KSA number from *ACSM's Guidelines for Exercise Testing and Prescription* (ACSM, 1995) to help you identify the objective of the question, and one or more appropriate references, with page numbers, for further study.

- Divide your study time into manageable units. You can accomplish this by concentrating on one KSA category at a time.

- In appendix A we have supplied a practice Health/Fitness Instructor examination. You can use this examination in one of two ways. One option is to use it as a pretest to help you identify your strengths and weaknesses within each of the KSA categories. Another option is to work through this study guide by answering the study questions presented in chapters 4-15 and then use the practice examination as a posttest.

REFERENCES

ACSM. (1994). *American College of Sports Medicine health/fitness instructor study packet.* Indianapolis: Author.

ACSM. (1995). *ACSM's guidelines for exercise testing and prescription* (5th ed.). Baltimore: Williams & Wilkins.

ACSM. (1996). *ACSM health/fitness instructor certification study packet.* Baltimore: Williams & Wilkins.

Howley, E.T., & Franks, B.D. (1992). *Health fitness instructor's handbook* (2nd ed.). Champaign, IL: Human Kinetics.

CHAPTER 2

The Written Examination

© Mary Langenfeld

The written examination is designed to assess your ability to recall and apply facts as defined by the ACSM KSAs. These KSAs are located in appendix F in the text titled *ACSM's Guidelines for Exercise Testing and Prescription* (ACSM, 1995).

EXAMINATION FORMAT AND NUMBER OF QUESTIONS

The written examination consists of approximately 100 multiple-choice questions. Each multiple-choice question will consist of a stem (the question) followed by four *(a-d)* or five *(a-e)* possible answers (options). Table 2.1 indicates the number of questions that you are likely to encounter in each of the examination categories.

TIME LIMIT AND SCORING

You will have a maximum of three hours to take the written examination. As a general rule of thumb, you should spend no more than one minute answering any one question. Questions that require you to perform mathematical calculations—most notably those that require you to solve metabolic equations as discussed in chapter 14—are an exception. The overall point is that you should not spend too much time pondering any single question. Instead, leave a blank for that question and plan to return to it after you have answered all the other questions.

Each multiple-choice question has only one correct answer. Therefore your answer will be scored either correct or incorrect. There is no penalty for guessing, and all questions are of equal weight.

TEST-TAKING SUGGESTIONS

Here are a few test-taking suggestions that will help improve your score:

- Read each question carefully, taking time to underline any key terms.
- Attempt, in your own mind, to answer each question before looking at the choices. Use your hand to cover up the choices.
- If your answer is not among the choices given, attempt to eliminate answers that you are confident are incorrect. This will

Table 2.1 Potential Distribution of Test Questions for the Written Examination

Examination category	Number of questions*
Functional Anatomy and Biomechanics	9
Exercise Physiology	15
Human Development and Aging	3
Pathophysiology and Risk Factors	6
Human Behavior and Psychology	4
Health Appraisal and Fitness Testing	12
Emergency Procedures and Safety	8
Exercise Programming	11
Nutrition and Weight Management	15
Program Administration and Management**	10
Metabolic Calculations	10

*Potential number of questions based on previous examinations that are reported to have contained 103 questions.

**Program Administration and Management questions encompass issues spanning all other KSAs and exercise leadership issues as well. You will find questions from this category in all other sections, and issues from all other categories in the questions in this section.

greatly increase your odds of selecting (or in some cases guessing) the correct answer.

- If you are uncertain about an answer, skip that question and move on to the next question. However, place a large mark beside the question so that you can easily come back to it later on.

- Since you will not be penalized for guessing, never leave a question blank. Always select one of the potential multiple-choice answers.

- Check your answer sheet to be sure you have not inadvertently left out a response.

TEST-TAKING PRECAUTIONS

At one time or another we have all been exposed to a poorly constructed teacher-made test in which an answer is so obvious that it nearly jumps off the test and onto the answer sheet. Don't expect this to be the case with your written certification examination. Indeed, the ACSM Health/Fitness Instructor written certification examination is a skillfully constructed assessment instrument. Outlined here are a couple of special precautions that you should keep in mind to improve your score.

▲ Be aware that a number of the questions on your written certification examination will require multiple thought processes. For example, compare the thought processes associated with these two questions:

1. The amount of blood ejected from the left ventricle with each beat is referred to as

   a. cardiac index
   b. cardiac output
   c. ejection fraction
   d. stroke volume

2. Mary is a 40-year-old female with a resting HR of 78 beats per minute and a maximal HR of 183 beats per minute. Using the HRR method, identify Mary's target HR when intensity is established as 70 percent of HRR.

   a. 126 beats per minute

   b. 142 beats per minute

   c. a 15-second pulse of 38 beats

   d. a 10-second pulse of 15 beats

The correct answer to the first question is d, stroke volume. This first question required just one simple thought process. In comparison, the second question is more difficult since it requires you to carry out several mental functions to derive the correct response. You will encounter both kinds of questions on the examination, so be on your toes.

Let's examine the thought processes needed to correctly answer the second question. First, you had to recall the HRR or Karvonen formula. You then had to extract the important information from the question to substitute into the formula (HR max = 183 beats per minute; resting HR = 78 beats per minute; 70 percent exercise intensity). You then mathematically solved the formula. You could see quickly that your answer of 152 beats per minute was not listed among the possible answers. You then had to convert responses *c* and *d* to beats per minute. Now you could see that *c*, a 15-second pulse of 38 beats, was the correct answer ($4 \times 38 = 152$ beats per minute).

Furthermore, had you selected the inappropriate rule-of-thumb formula (HR max = 220 – age), you would have incorrectly selected answer *a* ($220 - 40 = 180 \times .70 = 126$ beats per minute). As should be evident, the test writers for this examination are well aware of the mistakes people most commonly make for a given question. This knowledge allows them to include such incorrect responses among the available options. For this reason, don't rush into selecting an answer thinking that you must be correct because it appears among the possible responses. Instead, take your time and think through the logic underlying each question.

▲ Pay close attention to units of measure and location of decimal points. You may confront a list of potential answers that at first glance look similar but in reality are different. An example of this is a question with the answers 25 L, 2.5 L, .25 L, 25 ml, 2.5 ml, and .25 ml.

After you have completed the entire written examination, revisit any unanswered questions. Then if time remains, it is advisable to check over any questions that required you to perform mathematical calculations. However, avoid the temptation to change previously answered questions without thinking through your rationale for wanting to make the change.

REFERENCES

ACSM. (1995). *ACSM's guidelines for exercise testing and prescription* (5th ed.). Baltimore: Williams & Wilkins.

CHAPTER 3

The Practical Examination

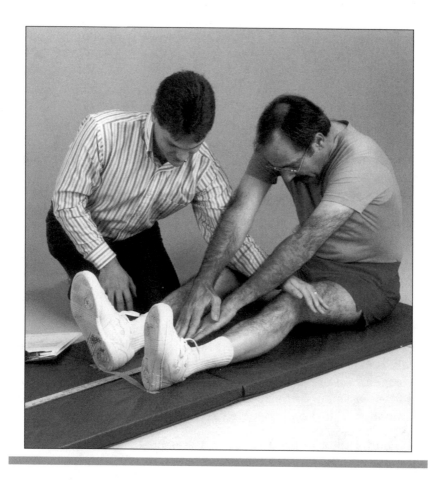

While the written examination is specifically designed to test your knowledge of the ACSM KSAs, the practical examination is specifically designed to test your ability to apply this knowledge as would be required in a real-world setting. In other words, the emphasis of the practical examination is not only on knowing what to do, but also on being able to carry out a defined task appropriately. In this chapter we discuss the format of the practical examination and describe, in some detail, tasks that you should practice and master before taking your certification examination.

EXAMINATION FORMAT

The practical is divided into four examination stations. Certification candidates are randomly assigned an initial station and will rotate through the remaining three. Upon entering an examination station, you will be greeted by an ACSM-certified examiner. The examiner is specifically trained to ask a series of prepared questions and/or describe to you a scenario to which you must respond. You will be allotted a maximum of 15 minutes at each of the four stations.

When responding to an examiner's question or scenario, you must adhere to one very important assumption. Namely, while your examiner will be knowledgeable and well trained, you must nevertheless gear your responses as if you were communicating with a client who possesses little knowledge regarding the subject matter in question.

THE FOUR PRACTICAL EXAMINATION STATIONS

Here we give a brief description of each of the four practical examination stations along with a list of tasks you may be asked to perform.

Station 1

The first station is designed to assess your knowledge and abilities in the areas of (1) anthropometric measurement, (2) body composition assessment, (3) exercise demonstration and exercise modification, and (4) assessment of flexibility. In part, to prepare for this area of examination you should be able to

- identify standardized skinfold assessment sites as outlined on page 56 of the ACSM's guidelines manual (1995). Your examiner may name a specific site, requiring you to appropriately identify and assess this area using standard skinfold calipers.

- identify standardized circumferential sites as outlined on page 58 of the ACSM guidelines manual (1995). Your examiner may name a specific site, requiring you to appropriately identify and assess this area using a Gulick or cloth tape.

- demonstrate and administer the sit-and-reach test protocol, adhering to the standards outlined on page 83 of the ACSM guidelines manual (1995).

- describe and demonstrate a flexibility exercise for a specific muscle group. Here your examiner may name a muscle group, requiring you to select and demonstrate an appropriate flexibility exercise. We suggest that you consult the chapter titled "Stretching and Warm-up" by Allerheilign, which you will find on pages 289-313 in the book edited by Baechle (1994). Another excellent source to consult is the work of Alter (1990).

Station 2

The second station is designed to assess your knowledge and abilities with respect to administering a test of muscular endurance. In addition, your exercise leadership skills in demonstrating and modifying resistance-training exercises will be assessed. In part, to prepare for this area of examination, you should be able to

- explain and demonstrate the push-up endurance test protocol as discussed on page 82 in the ACSM guidelines manual (1995). As with any muscular resistance activity, keep a watchful eye on the participant to ensure that he or she does not exhibit breath-holding. You must also insist that a person maintain correct form and technique at all times when performing any resistance-training exercise.

- demonstrate various resistance-training exercises for all the major muscle groups. We suggest that you consult Baechle (1994), especially chapter 21, pages 345-400. This source describes and illustrates 39 strength-training exercises, highlighting the body region being trained.

Station 3

The third station is designed to assess your knowledge, skills, and abilities with respect to preparation for a physical work capacity

(PWC) test. In part, to prepare for this area of examination you should be able to

- discuss emergency procedures (ACSM, 1995, pp. 253-262; ACSM, 1993, pp. 364-377), discuss preparation of the testing environment (ACSM, 1993, pp. 229-232), and discuss preparation of testing equipment including calibration (ACSM, 1993, pp. 229-232, 546-549).

- appropriately explain an informed consent. In your explanation be sure to address each of the six important components contained in an informed consent. Consult the ACSM guidelines manual (1995), pages 43-44, for a general informed consent form.

- explain to a client the purpose for using, and describe how to use, the Rating of Perceived Exertion (RPE) scale. Consult the ACSM guidelines manual (1995), pages 67-68, for an explanation and a copy of the RPE scale.

- properly adjust a cycle ergometer in preparation for an exercise test. Pay attention to point #3 of the ACSM "Standardized Guidelines for Submaximal Cardiovascular Evaluation" on page 70 in the ACSM guidelines manual (1995). Be prepared to demonstrate how you can adjust the ergometer's seat to accomplish a 5-degree bend at the knee joint when the pedal is at the endpoint in the downstroke.

- obtain a preexercise HR.

- obtain a preexercise BP.

Station 4

The fourth station is designed to assess your ability to administer a submaximal PWC test performed on a cycle ergometer. You will not be required to administer an entire test, only selected portions. As you enter this examination station a client may be in the midst of a PWC test and you will be instructed to proceed with the test. You will be told what protocol is being administered. One of two protocols will be employed—the YMCA Cycle Ergometry Protocol, which is reproduced in the ACSM guidelines manual (1995, p. 69), or the ACSM Cycle Ergometry Protocol (see Howley & Franks, 1992). Be sure to conduct the test in accordance with established guidelines as outlined on page 70 of the ACSM guidelines manual (1995). During test administration, you must be prepared to

- adjust workload at the appropriate time and to the appropriate level;
- measure HR, BP, and RPE at the appropriate times;
- know when to terminate the test;
- keep a watchful eye on the participant, looking for inappropriate changes in appearance and/or the presence of abnormal symptoms; and
- periodically ask the participant, "Are you feeling OK?"

SPECIAL ARRANGEMENTS FOR INDIVIDUALS WITH DISABILITIES

As should now be evident, the practical examination requires the candidate to demonstrate accurately various tasks. ACSM recognizes that individuals with disabilities may not be physically capable of performing some selected certification tasks. Therefore, ACSM will make special arrangements for individuals with disabilities so as not to exclude, segregate, or treat anyone differently from any other certification candidate. If you have a disability which requires special auxiliary aids or services as identified in the Americans with Disability Act, you should contact the ACSM National Office (317-637-9200) and request a copy of the form titled, "A Special Note for the Disabled." On this form you will be asked to describe your disability and any special equipment or situational needs. You should then return the form, along with written verification of your disability from a qualified professional, to the ACSM National Office no later than 30 days (preferably as soon as possible) before your workshop and/or certification date. A copy of the form and letter of disability verification should also be sent directly to your scheduled workshop/certification site. ACSM will notify you of any approved arrangements.

PREPARATION STRATEGIES

As we mentioned in the introduction, it is important that you practice and master the tasks outlined in this chapter before attempting certification. We suggest that approximately three to six months before the certification examination you make arrangements to practice these tasks under the supervision of a trained professional. Volunteer internships are frequently available in community fitness programs and in college-, corporate-, and hospital-sponsored fitness programs.

While working under the supervision of a trained professional as you practice, you should strive to collect anthropometric measurements, both skinfolds and circumferential measurements, on at least 75 to 100 individuals. To check your accuracy, ask the trained professional to perform these measurements also, and compare your measurements with those of the trained professional.

Other important ways you can prepare include leading a group exercise class through both a warm-up and a cooldown cycle, administering the sit-and-reach test and the push-up endurance test to at least 75 to 100 individuals, explaining and demonstrating appropriate resistance-training exercises to at least 50 individuals, and administering at least 50 submaximal cycle ergometry tests using the protocols outlined in this chapter. With appropriate practice, your confidence will increase and your anxiety regarding this phase of the certification examination will diminish.

REFERENCES

ACSM. (1993). *ACSM's resource manual for guidelines for exercise testing and prescription* (2nd ed.). Malvern, PA: Lea & Febiger.

ACSM. (1995). *ACSM's guidelines for exercise testing and prescription* (5th ed.). Baltimore: Williams & Wilkins.

Alter, M.J. (1990). *Sport stretch.* Champaign, IL: Human Kinetics.

Baechle, T.R. (Ed.) (1994). *Essentials of strength training and conditioning.* Champaign, IL: Human Kinetics.

Howley, E.T., & Franks, B.D. (1992). *Health fitness instructor's handbook* (2nd ed.). Champaign, IL: Human Kinetics.

PART
2

EXAMINATION STUDY QUESTIONS

CHAPTER 4

Functional Anatomy and Biomechanics

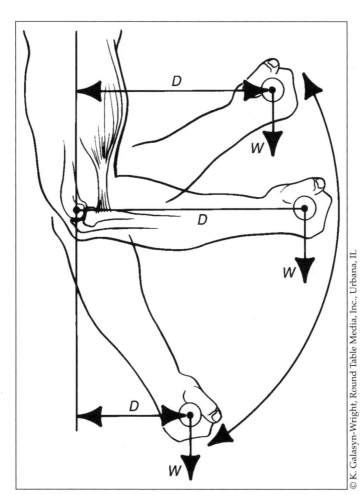

This ACSM KSA category, Functional Anatomy and Biomechanics, consists of 15 objectives, each containing multiple elements. While you may have only about nine questions from this category on your certification examination, we have constructed 82 practice questions to help you prepare for such a major content area. You should consult the textbooks cited at the end of this chapter, as they will provide you with the knowledge base you will need to pass this KSA category.

PRACTICE QUESTIONS

> Directions: Each question is followed by either four or five possible answers. Select the *best* answer to the question.

 1. The bones of the ischium, pubis, and vertebrae are classified as what type of bone?

   a. long

   b. flat

   c. short

   d. irregular

 2. What is indicated by an ossified epiphyseal plate located between the diaphysis and epiphysis of a long bone?

   a. The bone can no longer increase in length.

   b. The area around the plate is dead.

   c. The diameter of the bone will decrease.

   d. The bone is in a stage of growth.

   3. Generally, by what age are the majority of the bones in the human body ossified?

   a. 3-6 years

   b. 7-11 years

   c. 12-25 years

   d. 35 years

_C_   4. Which of the following shapes of bones and corresponding examples are *not* correctly matched?

    a. short bones–carpals, tarsals

    b. long bones–humerus, ulna

    c. flat bones–ethmoid, femur

    d. irregular bones–vertebrae, ilium

_B_   5. Of the following connective tissue types, which is found on the articulating surfaces of long bones?

    a. elastic cartilage

    b. hyaline cartilage

    c. reticular tissue

    d. dense irregular collagenous tissue

_D_   6. Of the following pairs of articulations, which pair is *not* correctly matched?

    a. synarthroses–fibrous

    b. amphiarthroses–cartilaginous

    c. diarthroses–pivot

    d. synovial–synchondrosis

_C_   7. A muscle fiber is a single cell consisting of all but which of the following components?

    a. sarcolemma

    b. sarcoplasm

    c. cilia

    d. myofibrils

_D_   8. Which of the following best describes myosin molecules?

    a. Myosin molecules consist of a double helix of F-actin, tropomyosin, and troponin.

    b. Myosin molecules run through the sarcolemma toward the T tubules.

    c. Myosin molecules separate the presynaptic terminal from the postsynaptic terminal.

    d. Myosin molecules consist of two globular heads and a rodlike filament.

_A_   9. What is the term for the outermost layer of connective tissue on the skeletal muscle?

   a. epimysium

   b. sarcomysium

   c. endomysium

   d. perimysium

_B_   10. What major characteristic distinguishes connective tissue from other tissue?

   a. mechanism of secretion

   b. extracellular matrix

   c. important function in diffusion

   d. ability to conduct electrical impulses

X _D_   11. Of the following connective tissue types, which is found within the lymph nodes, spleen, and bone marrow?

   _C_

   a. elastic cartilage

   b. hyaline cartilage

   c. reticular tissue

   d. dense irregular collagenous tissue

_A_   12. What makes up the extracellular matrix of cartilage?

   a. protein filaments and proteoglycan aggregates

   b. minerals

   c. fluid

   d. blood vessels

X _A_   13. Which of the following is *not* considered connective tissue?

   _B_ a. blood

   b. stratified epithelium

   c. bone

   d. adipose tissue

X _C_   14. Where are the SA node and the AV node located?

   _A_ a. the right atrium

   b. the right ventricle

   c. the right atrium and right ventricle, respectively

   d. the left atrium

_D_ 15. Of the following statements, which is *not* true of cardiac muscle cells?

   a. Cardiac muscle cells are similar in design to skeletal muscle cells.

   b. Cardiac muscle cells are joined by intercalated discs.

   c. Cardiac muscle cells are well supplied with blood vessels.

   d. Cardiac muscle cells contain a well-developed T-tubule system.

_A_ 16. Which of the following is a true statement about the heart?

   a. It contains a fibrous pericardium that holds it in place.

   b. It is composed of two ventricles separated by an inter-atrial septum.

   c. It has an endomysium, perimysium, and epimysium forming its wall.

   d. It is supplied by coronary arteries branching off the right and left subclavian arteries.

_A_ 17. Which of the following is true regarding the external anatomy of the heart?

   a. Each atria has a flap of tissue called an auricle.

   b. The aorta exits the right ventricle.

   c. The four pulmonary veins enter the right atrium.

   d. The pulmonary trunk exits the left ventricle.

_C_ 18. Deoxygenated blood returning from the body enters the superior and inferior venae cavae. What is the correct sequence of events for blood flow through the heart?

   a. right atrium, right ventricle, pulmonary arteries, tricuspid valve

   b. right atrium, mitral valve, right ventricle, pulmonary veins

   c. right atrium, tricuspid valve, right ventricle, pulmonary arteries

   d. right atrium, mitral valve, right ventricle, pulmonary veins

X   A   19. Which of the following is true of coronary circulation?

C   a. A large coronary sinus separates the right and left ventricles.

b. The left coronary artery and the right anterior interventricular artery arise from the sinus of Valsalva.

c. The right circumflex artery eventually anastomoses with the circumflex artery.

d. The right coronary artery gives rise to the circumflex arteries.

X   D   20. Blood functions include all but which of the following?

B   a. transporting gases, nutrients, and waste products

b. providing ATP for cellular metabolism

c. aiding in pH maintenance

d. protecting against disease

A   21. Which of the following is true of blood vessels?

a. Valves prevent backflow of blood in the veins.

b. All blood vessels have three layers.

c. Veins have many elastic fibers and a large amount of smooth muscle.

d. Blood flow to an organ is regulated by the action of precapillary sphincters in the arteries.

D   22. The trachea extends from which of the following?

a. larynx to pharynx

b. nose to pharynx

c. pharynx to primary bronchi

d. larynx to primary bronchi

X   D   23. Functionally, the respiratory system is divided into which of the following?

C   a. conducting zone structures, respiratory zone structures, and diaphragmatic breathing zones

b. passages that filter, warm, and moisten incoming air; and upper and lower breathing zones

    c. conducting zone structures; passages that filter, warm, and moisten incoming air; and respiratory zone structures

    d. respiratory zone structures and upper and lower breathing zones

C 24. Which of the following is an accurate statement about the larynx?

    a. It is an organ of both the respiratory system and digestive system located at the back of the oral and nasal cavities.

    b. It helps to filter air.

    c. It is also called the voice box, which contains the vocal cords.

    d. It is located between the phalanx and pharynx.

C 25. How many lobes does the right lung have?

    a. one

    b. two

    c. three

    d. four

C 26. Besides the ribs and costal cartilages, what is (are) contained in the thoracic cage?

    a. diaphragm

    b. sternum and diaphragm

    c. sternum and intercostals

    d. sternum and vertebrae

C 27. Which of the following statements is true of the vertebral column?

    a. Each thoracic vertebra contains a peglike projection called the dens, or odontoid process, for articulation with the ribs.

    b. The lumbar vertebrae are easily identified by their long spinous processes and fovea for articulation with the ribs.

    c. The 12 thoracic vertebrae have transverse foramina and long, downward spinous processes.

    d. The seven cervical vertebrae have transverse foramina.

28. Which of the following is true of the appendicular skeleton?
    a. It consists of upper and lower limbs and the girdles that attach to the limbs.
    b. It consists of the skull, vertebrae, thoracic cage, and shoulder girdle.
    c. It consists of the bones that form the axis of the body.
    d. It supports and protects the organs of the head, neck, and trunk.

29. Which of the following is true of the major bones of the body?
    a. The mandible and maxilla possess alveolar processes with sockets for the attachment ossicles of the middle ear.
    b. Eight tarsal bones make up the ankle.
    c. The occipital bone forms the lower sides of the cranium and contains a mastoid process that is easily palpated behind the earlobe.
    d. The femur articulates with the head of the coxa, the medial and lateral condyles of the tibia, and the patella.

30. Which of the following best describes the trapezius?
    a. It inserts at the clavicle, acromion process, and scapular spine; and elevates, depresses, retracts, and fixes the scapula.
    b. It is innervated by the subclavian nerve; and elevates, depresses, retracts, and fixes the scapula.
    c. It originates at the first to the ninth ribs and adducts and abducts the upper arm.
    d. It inserts at the sternum, clavicle, and acromion process and adducts and abducts the upper arm.

31. Of the following, which is (are) true about the pectoralis major?
    a. It adducts, flexes, and medially rotates the arm.
    b. It inserts on the greater tubercle of the humerus.
    c. It is innervated by the axillary nerve.
    d. *a* and *b* only
    e. *a*, *b*, and *c*

32. Compression of the abdomen is accomplished by the external obliques and which of the following muscles?

    a. pectoralis major, rectus abdominis, transverse abdominis

    b. rectus abdominis, internal abdominal obliques, transverse abdominis

    c. rectus abdominis, diaphragm, internal abdominal obliques

    d. transverse abdominis, internal abdominal obliques, diaphragm

33. Which of the following is (are) true of the erector spinae muscles?

    a. They originate as a large fleshy mass in the sacral area of the back.

    b. They consist of the iliocostalis, longissimus, and the spinalis muscles.

    c. They extend the vertebral column and flex the hip.

    d. *a* and *b* only

    e. *a*, *b*, and *c*

34. Which of the following is (are) true about the gluteus maximus?

    a. It contributes most of the mass of the buttocks.

    b. It abducts and laterally rotates the thigh.

    c. It flexes the thigh.

    d. *a* and *b* only

    e. *a*, *b*, and *c*

35. Which muscles are involved in thigh extension?

    a. the gluteus medius

    b. the hamstrings

    c. the semitendinosus, biceps femoris, and the semimembranosus

    d. *a* and *b* only

    e. *a*, *b*, and *c*

36. Which movements are associated with the gastrocnemius?
   a. extending the four lateral toes and flexing the leg
   b. plantar flexion of the foot and flexing the leg
   c. extending the four lateral toes and extending the great toe
   d. plantar flexion of the foot and extending the great toe

37. Which of the following combinations would result in pronation of the subtalar joint?
   a. eversion and abduction
   b. eversion and adduction
   c. inversion and abduction
   d. inversion and adduction

38. From the anatomical position, what are the two primary movements occurring in the sagittal plane in addition to flexion?
   a. extension and rotation
   b. extension and hyperextension
   c. extension and adduction
   d. extension and hyperflexion

39. What movement returns a body segment to the anatomical position?
   a. flexion
   b. extension
   c. inversion
   d. eversion

40. What action moves a body segment away from the midline of the body?
   a. flexion
   b. extension
   c. abduction
   d. adduction

C 41. What movements occur within the frontal plane?

    a. flexion, extension, rotation

    b. flexion, abduction, adduction

    c. inversion, abduction, adduction

    d. medial and lateral rotation

D 42. What name is given to movement beyond the anatomical position when starting from a position of flexion?

    a. abduction

    b. extension

    c. hyperflexion

    d. hyperextension

 C 43. The movement of what parts of the body is described by left and right rotation?

B

    a. thigh, leg, and foot

    b. head, neck, and trunk

    c. head and neck

    d. trunk, hip, and foot

B 44. An example of what movement(s) is produced by the circular movement of a limb?

    a. circumcision

    b. circumduction

    c. circumflexion

    d. circumvention

    e. *a* and *b* only

 D 45. Of these pairs of joint classifications and associated movements, which one is correct?

C

    a. synarthrodial–slightly movable

    b. amphiarthrodial–immovable

    c. diarthrodial–freely movable

    d. synovial–slightly movable

X <u>B</u> 46. Which of the following joint types is not a synovial joint?

D
    a. ellipsoid

    b. hinge

    c. pivot

    d. synchondrosis

X <u>D</u> 47. Which of the following is a true statement about fibrous joints?

A
    a. They have no joint cavity and include sutures, syndesmoses, and gomphoses.

    b. They have no joint cavity and include bursae and synchondroses.

    c. They are incapable of any movement.

    d. They contain hyaline cartilage between bone segments.

X <u>A</u> 48. Which of the following is a true statement about cartilaginous joints?

C
    a. They are freely movable.

    b. They contain a synovial membrane.

    c. They could be identified with the symphysis pubis.

    d. They include sutures, gomphoses, and syndesmoses.

<u>C</u> 49. Which of the following best describes synovial joints?

    a. They are slightly movable and have an articular cartilage on the ends of the bone.

    b. They are slightly movable and include symphyses.

    c. They have an articular cartilage on the ends of the bones and a synovial membrane that produces synovial fluid.

    d. They include symphyses and have a synovial membrane that produces synovial fluid.

X <u>B</u> 50. Which of the following statements is true of stability?

D
    a. The smaller the base of support, the more stable the body.

b. Movement toward the midline of the body in one direction will cause the center of gravity to shift away from that direction, making the body more stable.

c. A foot position that allows for a small base of support in the direction of the movement will provide added stability.

d. Stability is directly proportional to the distance of the line of gravity from the limits of the base of support.

51. What is an individual's ability to control equilibrium called?

a. stability

b. balance

c. static motion

d. torque

52. When is the body's ability to maintain equilibrium enhanced?

a. when opposing forces acting on the body are not equal

b. when the center of gravity is vertically positioned near the edge of the base of support

c. when body mass is increased and the base of support is directed in the line of action of the external force

d. when the friction between the body and the surface area is decreased

53. Which of the following paired terms indicate abnormal back curvatures commonly called "hunched back" and "hollow back," respectively?

a. lordosis–kyphosis

b. kyphosis–lordosis

c. scoliosis–lordosis

d. lordosis–scoliosis

54. What is scoliosis?

a. a lateral deviation of the spine

b. an anterior exaggeration of the lumbar curve

c. exaggerated posterior thoracic convexity

d. exaggerated posterior lumbar concavity

55. Which of the following is true about most cases of low-back pain?

    a   It is in the diagnosis of less than 1 percent of all chronic health problems.

    b. It is usually accompanied by kidney infection.

    c. It is generally caused by psychological stress.

    d. It accounts for more lost person-hours than any other occupational injury.

56. What exercises are recommended for low-back pain?

    a. sit-ups with knees extended followed by sit-ups with knees in flexion

    b. leg lifts and sit-ups with knees in flexion

    c. sit-ups (crunches) with knees in flexion

    d. leg lifts and aerobic exercise

57. What exercise is often neglected in low-back health?

    a. ballistic back hyperextension exercises with ROM past normal standing lumbar lordosis

    b. back extension exercises with ROM limited to normal standing lumbar lordosis

    c. partial sit-up with the lumbar spine kept in contact with the floor

    d. full sit-up with feet supported

58. What result can be expected when one carries light (< 0.45 kilograms) hand weights while exercising?

    a. increase in metabolic energy expenditure by a large percentage (> 20 percent)

    b. increase in the risk of injury to the shoulder

    c. reduction in ROM at the elbow and shoulder

    d. increase in ROM for individuals with arthritis

59. What protocols are included in training programs designed to improve strength?

    a. isometric

    b. isotonic with constant or varying resistance

    c. isokinetic

    d. all of the above

X _B_ 60. What name is given to an exercise designed to develop
        strength that puts a muscle group on stretch prior to its
  C   contraction?

    a. repetitions maximum

    b. isokinetic

    c. plyometric

    d. progressive resistive

_B_ 61. For optimal strength gains, a typical weight-training pro-
       gram would include which of the following?

    a. one set of bicep curls with 10-pound weights, one day a
       week, for ten weeks

    b. three sets of exercises with 6-10 RM protocol

    c. one set of exercises with 20 RM protocol

    d. lift one time per week

    e. adhere to the overload principle

_D_ 62. Which of the following approaches is (are) recommended to
       improve flexibility?

    a. Increase the strength of the antagonistic muscle and
       decrease the resistance of the tight musculature.

    b. Employ a technique of static stretching.

    c. Employ a technique called proprioceptive neuro-
       muscular facilitation.

    d. b and c only

X _C_ 63. What are the quality points to look for in the sit and reach
       test?

    a. tight hamstrings

    b. tight low back

    c. stretched upper back

    d. a and b only

    e. a, b, and c

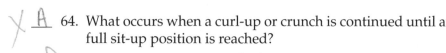

64. What occurs when a curl-up or crunch is continued until a full sit-up position is reached?
  a. movement occurs at the hip joint
  b. the psoas and iliacus muscles become prime movers
  c. abdominals are strengthened
  d. a and b only
  e. a, b, and c

65. Match the type of joint and corresponding movement associated with the shoulder.
  a. gliding–hyperextension
  b. pivot–pronation
  c. ball and socket–circumduction
  d. hinge–flexion

66. Which of the following describes the type of joint in which the articulating surfaces are nearly flat and where the only movement allowed is a monoaxial motion confined to one plane?
  a. pivot
  b. gliding
  c. condyloid
  d. ball and socket

67. Choose the correctly matched type of joint, corresponding movement, and example.
  a. gliding–nonaxial gliding–facets of the vertebrae
  b. saddle–circumduction–knee
  c. ginglymus–flexion–shoulder
  d. pivot–biaxial rotation–elbow

68. Where might you find a joint that has one convex articulating bone surface and one concave articulating bone surface with movement restricted to a hinge-like motion?
  a. knee
  b. neck

c. shoulder

d. hip

69. The intertarsal joints allow which of the following movements?

a. plantar flexion and dorsiflexion

b. horizontal flexion and horizontal extension

c. pronation and supination

d. combination pronation and abduction; combination supination and abduction

70. What movements are included in frontal plane movements of the hip?

a. lateral flexion and adduction

b. adduction and abduction

c. lateral flexion and lateral extension

d. adduction and lateral extension

71. What movements are included in the transverse plane movements of the forearm?

a. outward and inward rotation

b. pronation and supination

c. medial and lateral rotation

d. eversion and inversion

e. a and c

72. The degree of movement within a specific joint (ROM) is limited by which of the following?

a. bony structures of two articulating surfaces

b. length of the ligaments

c. elasticity of the connective tissues

d. all of the above

73. What is the term for the fluid force that enables flotation?

a. drag

b. lift

c. buoyancy

d. Magnus effect

_B_ 74. What is the term for the fluid force that acts to slow a cyclist moving through that fluid?

a. turbulence

b. drag

c. lift

d. friction

_D_ 75. Propulsion in swimming results from a complex interplay of what two fluid forces?

a. Magnus effect and drag

b. skin friction and wave drag

c. propulsive lift and loft

d. propulsive lift and propulsive drag

_A_ 76. Which of the following biomechanical principles are applicable when one lifts a heavy object?

a. establishing a base of support as close as possible to the load being carried and lowering the body into position by flexing the knees, hips, and ankles

b. stabilizing the vertebral column in the flexed position and lowering the body into position by flexing at the waist

c. stabilizing the vertebral column in the flexed position and raising the load with the extensor muscles of the legs

d. establishing a base of support as far as possible from the load being carried and lowering the body into position by flexing the knees, hips, and ankles

_A_ 77. When a load is carried, which of the following biomechanical considerations would be true?

D   a. It is good body mechanics to keep the body erect, with the head and spine carried in the midsagittal plane of the body.

b. The body's balance remains more stable when the object is carried close to the edge of the base of support.

    c. The body segments can be moved in a direction toward the load to improve balance.

    d. Laterally flexing the vertebral column will produce the desired balancing countertorque when an object (e.g., a suitcase) is carried with one arm.

B 78. Forward speed during walking and running results from what two elements?

    a. vertical force and time of ground contact

    b. stride length and stride frequency

    c. stride frequency and vertical push

    d. stride length and horizontal lift

B 79. During walking, the foot applies a force to the ground and there follows an equal and opposite ground reaction force to the foot. This is an example of which of Newton's laws of motion?

    a. first

    b. second

    c. third

    d. fourth

C 80. Which of the following is (are) true regarding variable-resistance weight-training machines?

    a. They maintain the force generated by a muscle and allow for the change in joint angle throughout the ROM.

    b. They allow for the change in joint angle and accommodate the changing moment arms of the muscle to match the maximal torques of that muscle group throughout the ROM.

    c. They maintain a constant velocity without regard to resistance force and maintain the force generated by a muscle throughout the ROM.

    d. *a* and *b* only

    e. *a*, *b*, and *c*

81. Which statement correctly identifies the measurement site for biacromial breadth?

a. distance between the most medial and most lateral aspects of the femoral condyles

b. distance between the most medial and most lateral aspects of the humeral epicondyles

c. most lateral borders of the acromion processes

d. most lateral borders of the greater tubercles of the humerus

82. What is the correct anatomic landmark site for determining pulse?

a. femoral pulse–anterior thigh, posterior to the inguinal ligament, midway between the anterior superior iliac spine and the pubis symphysis

b. popliteal–deep within the patellar fossa

c. radial pulse–distal end of the ulna

d. *a* and *b*

REFERENCES FOR FURTHER STUDY

1. ACSM. (1993). *ACSM's resource manual for guidelines for exercise testing and prescription* (2nd ed.). Malvern, PA: Lea & Febiger.

2. Hall, S.J. (1995). *Basic biomechanics* (2nd ed.). St. Louis: Mosby.

3. Howley, E.T., & Franks, B.D. (1997). *Health fitness instructor's handbook* (3rd ed.). Champaign, IL: Human Kinetics.

4. Kreighbaum, E., & Barthels, K.M. (1990). *Biomechanics: A qualitative approach for studying movement* (3rd ed.). New York: Macmillan.

5. Seeley, R.R., Stephens, T.D., & Tate, P. (1995). *Anatomy & physiology* (3rd ed.). St. Louis: Mosby.

ANSWERS

Question number	Answer	KSA number	Reference	Page number
1	d	1	3	81
2	a	1	5	166, 177, 180

Question number	Answer	KSA number	Reference	Page number
3	c	1	5	177
4	c	1	3	81
5	b	1	5	165
6	d	1	5	237
7	c	1	5	282
8	d	1	5	285
9	a	1	5	282
10	b	1	5	117
11	c	1	5	122
12	a	1	5	125
13	b	1	5	119
14	a	2	5	643
			3	437
15	d	2	5	641
16	a	2	5	631
17	a	2	5	635
18	c	2	5	640
19	c	2	5	635
20	b	2	5	605
21	a	2	5	667
22	d	2	5	762
23	c	2	5	758
24	c	2	5	759
25	c	2	5	763
26	d	3	5	217
27	d	3	5	211

Question number	Answer	KSA number	Reference	Page number
28	a	3	5	219
29	d	3	5	227
30	a	3	5	338
31	d	3	5	340
32	b	3	5	333
33	d	3	5	331
34	d	3	5	350
35	e	3	5	351, 354
36	b	3	5	355
37	a	4	2	39
38	b	4	2	36
39	b	4	2	36
40	c	4	2	37
41	c	4	2	37
42	d	4	2	36
43	b	4	2	39
44	b	4	2	43
45	c	5	2	111
46	d	5	2	112
47	a	5	5	236
48	c	5	5	239
49	c	5	5	240
50	d	6	2	424
51	b	6	2	424
52	c	6	2	425
53	b	7	2	262

Question number	Answer	KSA number	Reference	Page number
54	a	7	2	263
55	d	8	2	284
56	c	8	3	329
57	b	8	1	54
58	c	9	1	42
59	d	10	3	295
			1	45
60	c	10	3	300
61	b	10	3	299
62	d	11	4	301
63	e	11	3	255
64	d	11	3	318
65	c	12	3	85
66	b	12	2	113
67	a	12	2	114
			5	242
68	a	12	5	242
69	d	12	3	89
70	b	12	2	38
71	e	12	2	39
72	d	13	3	84
73	c	14	2	469
74	b	14	2	470
75	d	14	2	488
76	a	14	4	327
77	d	14	4	327

Question number	Answer	KSA number	Reference	Page number
78	b	14	1	40
79	c	14	2	362
80	b	14	1	45
81	c	15	1	14
82	a	15	1	6

CHAPTER 5

Exercise Physiology

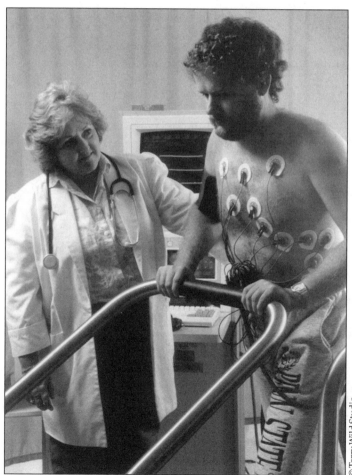

The ACSM KSA category titled Exercise Physiology contains 37 objectives. Objective #18 requires you to calculate metabolic problems, and because of the importance of metabolic equations on the examination, a separate section of the written examination is devoted specifically to the solving of metabolic equations. Chapter 14 of this book, which is a metabolic equation tutorial, will provide you with additional information and help prepare you for this special section of the written certification examination. Not counting metabolic equations, on the basis of previous ACSM Health/Fitness Instructor certification examinations you are likely to encounter approximately 15 questions from this KSA category.

PRACTICE QUESTIONS

Directions: Each question is followed by either four or five possible answers. Select the *best* answer to the question.

1. What is true about a metabolic process requiring no O_2?
    a. It is termed aerobic; could be written as $ATP \rightarrow ADP + Pi + Energy$.
    b. It is termed anaerobic; could be written as $ATP \rightarrow ADP + Pi + Energy$.
    c. It is found exclusively in the mitochondria of a cell.
    d. It is termed Krebs cycle; could be written as $CP + ADP \rightarrow ATP + C + Energy$.

X   ⌂   2. Which of the following statements is (are) true regarding
    No   aerobic metabolism?
    A
    a. It requires O_2; involves a mitochondrial process in which inorganic phosphate is coupled to ADP via the electron transport chain.
    b. It can utilize muscle glycogen, blood glucose, plasma free fatty acids, and intramuscular fats.
    c. It is useful for long-term activities; is the term commonly used to describe the level of O_2 consumption at which there is a rapid rise in blood lactate.
    d. *a and b*

_A_ 3. Generally, what contributes the most to intense activity and long-lasting activity, respectively?

   a. anaerobic sources–aerobic sources

   b. oxidation of fat–metabolism of glucose

   c. aerobic sources–anaerobic sources

   d. oxidation of glucose–the ATP-PC system

_C_ 4. Which of the following is (are) true about short-term, high-intensity exercise?

   a. Aerobic metabolism provides the primary source of ATP.

   b. A half-mile swim and the 1500-meter run are good examples.

   c. It typically lasts 5-60 seconds, and the ATP-PC system and anaerobic glycolysis are preferentially used to provide ATP.

   d. *b* and *c*

_D_ 5. What term refers to the volume of blood pumped through the aorta every minute?

   a. stroke volume

   b. ejection fraction

   c. end-systolic volume

   d. cardiac output

_B_ 6. What term refers to the body's ability to transport and utilize O_2 during rest or exercise?

   a. the respiratory exchange ratio

   b. $\dot{V}O_2$

   c. $\dot{V}O_2max$

   d. pulmonary ventilation

 _B_ 7. Which of the following is true regarding hyperventilation?

   a. It is increased pulmonary ventilation with a retention of carbon dioxide.

   b. It is due to an increase in expiration of air.

c. It occurs at approximately 40 percent $\dot{V}O_2$max.

d. It can lead to respiratory alkalosis without physiological compensation.

A 8. What term refers to the highest arterial BP recorded during the cardiac cycle?

a. SBP

b. DBP

c. mean arterial BP

d. total peripheral resistance

B 9. What is the pressure in the arterial system when the cardiac muscle is relaxed, and what is the normal value?

a. SBP; typically 120 mm Hg

b. DBP; typically 80 mm Hg

c. mean arterial pressure; typically 90 mm Hg

d. total peripheral resistance; typically 100 mm Hg

E 10. What is true about myocardial ischemia?

a. It is a condition of inadequate blood flow.

b. It may be accompanied by atherosclerosis.

c. It may have concomitant angina pectoris.

d. *a* and *b*

e. *a, b,* and *c*

D 11. What is true about tachycardia?

No a. It is exemplified by a HR greater than 100 beats per minute.

E b. It is a response to fever, nervous excitement, or exercise.

c. It acts to increase the O_2 delivered to the cells of the body via an increase in circulation.

d. *a* and *b*

e. *a, b,* and *c*

D 12. Which is true about bradycardia?

a. It is defined as a condition in which the HR is less than 60 beats per minute.

b. It is a condition that occurs during sleep and is seen in some physically fit people.

c. It is also called sick sinus syndrome.

d. *a* and *b*

e. *a, b,* and *c*

E 13. What is true about myocardial infarction?

a. It is also called heart attack.

b. It is death of a portion of the heart muscle.

c. It is caused by obstruction in a coronary artery due to atherosclerosis or embolism.

d. *a* and *b*

e. *a, b,* and *c*

A 14. What is true about angina pectoris?

a. It is a sudden pain in the chest area, most often due to a lack of O_2 to the heart tissue.

b. It is a painless episode of coronary insufficiency.

c. It is a tumor of the heart muscle.

d. It occurs quite often during exercise.

e. It is a thin, triangular muscle of the upper chest wall beneath the pectoralis major.

A 15. In general, what nutrient combination is used preferentially during high-intensity activity and metabolized preferentially during long-term activity, respectively?

a. CHO–FAT

b. FAT–CHO

c. FAT–PRO

d. PRO–FAT

X C 16. Which of the exercise prescriptions below meet the recom-
NO   mended cardiorespiratory fitness guidelines?
D
a. intensity = 50-85 percent $\dot{V}O_2$max; frequency = three times per week; duration = time required to expend 200 kcal

b. intensity = 50-85 percent HRR; frequency = three times per week; duration = 200 kcal per session

c. intensity = 50-60 percent HR max; frequency = three times per week; duration = 30 minutes per session

d. *a* and *b*

e. *a*, *b*, and *c*

17. An optimal program for strength training would include which of the following guidelines?

a. a minimum of 8-10 different exercises involving the major muscle groups

b. exercises that involve the full ROM

c. performance at an intensity level that would cause fatigue within 10-12 repetitions

d. *a, b,* and *c*

18. Which of the following describes the best training to improve flexibility?

a. static stretching; five sessions per week; holding each stretch for 60 seconds minimum

b. ballistic stretching; five sessions per week; holding each stretch for 1-2 seconds

c. static stretching; two sessions per week; holding each stretch for 10-60 seconds (depending upon flexibility training level)

d. a combination of static and ballistic stretching (dependent upon joint area); two sessions per week; repeating each stretch 10 times with no limit on stretch holding time

19. There is a great concern about body fat and its association with obesity and health-related problems. Which of the statements below identifies a component of fitness as it relates to body fat?

a. Recommended body fat percentages for men should fall between 12 and 18 percent.

b. Recommended body fat percentages for women should fall between 12 and 18 percent.

    c. A BMI of below 25 kg/m² is desirable.

    d. *a* and *b*

    e. *a, b,* and *c*

20. Which of the components listed accurately reflects the concept of motor fitness?

    a. speed–the ability to move quickly

    b. body composition–measured as a percentage of body fat

    c. agility–the ability to change direction quickly; and power–the rate of work where P = (F × d)/t

    d. *a* and *c*

21. During an acute bout of aerobic exercise, which of the following occur(s)?

    a. BP increases linearly with exercise intensity.

    b. HR increases linearly with exercise intensity.

    c. SV increases linearly with exercise intensity.

    d. *a* and *b*

    e. *a, b,* and *c*

22. Which of the following accurately describe(s) O₂ consumption?

    a. It increases linearly until a steady state is reached in a single bout of exercise.

    b. It increases linearly during graded exercise.

    c. It increases linearly over time during a steady state exercise bout.

    d. *a* and *b*

    e. *a, b,* and *c*

23. Which of the following occur(s) during an isometric grip strength test?

    a. SBP increases with a concomitant decrease in DBP.

    b. HR increases linearly until a steady state is reached.

    c. HR and DBP increase over time.

    d. *a* and *b*

__E__ 24. Which of the following occur(s) when a static contraction is performed at 60 percent MVC?

    a. Blood flow to the muscle is reduced.

    b. SBP may exceed 200 mm Hg.

    c. HR increases moderately.

    d. *a* and *b*

    e. *a, b,* and *c*

__E__ 25. What causes elevated O_2 levels observed during post-exercise?

    a. the replenishing of PC in the muscle and O_2 in the blood and tissues

    b. an elevated HR and BP

    c. physiological consequences as a result of elevated body temperature

    d. *a* and *b*

    e. *a, b,* and *c*

__D__ 26. What result would be expected for a given bout of exercise after a person engages in endurance training?

    a. an improved SV

    b. a lower HR

    c. an increased Q

    d. *a* and *b*

    e. *a, b,* and *c*

__A__ 27. Jay and Lynn began an exercise program together. They jogged at 75 percent of their $\dot{V}O_2$max, four times a week, for 30 minutes per session. After two months, they wondered what physiological changes may have occurred as a result of their training. Please note that Jay is 6 feet 1 inches and 180 pounds; Lynn is 5 feet 2 inches and 115 pounds. What cardiovascular changes would be expected after completion of their training program?

    a. Lynn's $\dot{V}O_2$max will be lower than Jay's $\dot{V}O_2$max.

    b. Jay's and Lynn's $\dot{V}O_2$max will be equal.

    c. Jay's BP will be increased at rest.

    d. Lynn's BP will be increased at rest.

_E_ 28. A female walks on a treadmill at a given speed and grade. Her HR is generally higher than that of her male counter-part at the same workload. What is (are) the reason(s) for the difference?

    a. the increased body fat of women

    b. lower hemoglobin in women

    c. smaller heart volume in women

    d. *a* and *b*

    e. *a, b,* and *c*

_D_ 29. What physiological adaptations occur as a result of strength training?

    a. an increase in muscle mass

    b. hypertrophy

    c. hyperplasia

    d. *a* and *b*

    e. *a, b,* and *c*

_E_ 30. What central nervous system adaptations result from a strength-training program?

    a. an increase in the number of motor units recruited

    b. a modification in the firing rates of motor units

    c. an enhancement in motor unit synchronization during a movement pattern

    d. a removal of neural inhibition

    e. all of the above

X _E_ 31. To what can we attribute the gains in strength that occur early (first three weeks) in a strength-training program?

    D a. an enlargement of the muscle

    b. hyperplasia

    c. hypertrophy

    d. neural adaptation

    e. all of the above

D 32. After a six-month progressive resistive-exercise strength-training program, which of the following will be noted in females when compared to a male counterpart?

    a. similar gains in relative strength

    b. less hypertrophy

    c. more atrophy

    d. *a* and *b*

    e. *a, b,* and *c*

E 33. According to research conducted thus far on resistance training, what are some of the early increases in voluntary strength attributable to?

    a. improved coordination

    b. improved learning

    c. increased activation of the prime mover muscles

    d. *a* and *b*

    e. *a, b,* and *c*

A 34. What occurs in the early stages of strength training?

    a. Muscle strength increases more than muscle size.

    b. Muscle size increases more than muscle strength.

    c. There is an increase in oxidative enzyme activities within the muscle.

    d. HR responses to work show little change.

D 35. What would be expected in a strength-training program conducted for 6 to 8 weeks?

B

    a. gains in strength due to muscle hypertrophy

    b. gains in strength due to neural adaptations

    c. an increase in the number of type IIa fibers

    d. *a* and *b*

    e. *a, b,* and *c*

E 36. Which of the following is (are) true about a MET?

    a. It is an estimate used to determine true physiological O_2 cost for work.

b. It is equal to 3.5 ml/kg/min.

c. It can be used to estimate functional capacity in a GXT.

d. *a* and *b*

e. *a, b,* and *c*

D 37. What is true about estimating caloric expenditure during exercise?

a. It can be determined using METs.

b. It is equal to METs × 3.5 × body weight.

c. It would be 10 kcal/min if the individual weighed 70 kilograms, was exercising at 6 METs, and had a weekly goal of 1,000 kcal expended for exercise.

d. *a* and *b*

e. *a, b,* and *c*

E 38. What is 1 MET?

a. a metabolic equivalent

b. a unit used to estimate the metabolic cost of physical activity relative to resting levels

c. 3.5 ml of O_2 consumption per kilogram of body weight

d. the resting metabolic rate

e. all of the above

D 39. What are the two most common sites for pulse palpation of HR during exercise?

a. brachial artery and carotid artery

b. radial artery and brachial artery

c. femoral artery and radial artery

d. carotid artery and radial artery

e. femoral artery and carotid artery

B 40. What is the preferred method for determining HR through palpation?

a. using the thumb at the radial site

b. using the fingers at the radial site

c. using the fingers on the carotid artery

d. applying enough pressure to trigger a reflex to slow the HR at the carotid site

_D_ 41. Why should caution be exercised when determining HR by palpating the carotid artery?

a. Palpating at this site requires a great deal of experience and should not be performed by a novice.

b. Palpating at this site is not as accurate as palpating at other sites and should be done only in an emergency situation.

c. Palpating at this site may initiate the baroreceptor reflex if pressure to the area is inadequate.

d. Palpating at this site may cause the HR to slow down if too much pressure is used.

_E_ 42. Which of the following is (are) true about warm-up activities before exercise?

a. They prepare the body for vigorous activity.

b. They may prevent injury.

c. They allow the body to redirect blood to the muscles.

d. They increase the elasticity of the connective tissue and other muscle components.

e. all of the above

X _D_ 43. Optimal warm-up prior to activity results in which of the following?

_E_ a. less muscle resistance when the warm-up is performed similarly to the activity (e.g., a baseball pitcher practicing at 60 percent of normal effort)

b. an increase in muscle enzyme reaction when muscle temperature is elevated

c. a possible lowering in the O_2 deficit at the onset of work

d. *a* and *b*

e. *a, b,* and *c*

X _D_ 44. What is (are) the primary physiological benefit(s) to be gained during a cooldown after exercise?

_E_ a. promoting a quicker return of HR and BP to normal values

b. stimulating the return of pooled blood from limbs to the central circulation

c. preventing the possibility of fainting

d. *a* and *b*

e. *a, b,* and *c*

B 45. Physiological benefits of warm-up include all but which of the following?

a. an increased breakdown of oxyhemoglobin to enhance O_2 delivery to the muscle

b. an inhibition of catecholamine release, perhaps preventing arrhythmias

c. an enhancement in enzyme activity, which lowers the energy of activation for improved cellular metabolic reactions

d. a reduction in the viscosity of muscle, thereby improving mechanical efficiency and power

e. a stimulation of earlier onset of sweating, which may reduce heat stress

X D 46. Which of the following is (are) true regarding an active cooldown period following exercise?

E

a. It enhances removal of catecholamines from the blood, which in susceptible individuals may prevent a cardiac arrhythmia.

b. It prevents blood pooling in the legs and thereby may prevent delayed muscle stiffening.

c. It promotes lactate utilization, which in turn hastens recovery.

d. *a* and *b*

e. *a, b,* and *c*

E 47. What might be the physiological consequences(s) to runners participating in a prolonged road race held on a morning when the wet bulb globe temperature was 75 degrees?

a. Blood flow will be distributed to the skin for cooling purposes, thus decreasing Q to the working muscle.

  b. End-diastolic volume may be reduced as a direct result of the shunting of blood to the periphery.

  c. A condition known as cardiovascular drift may occur.

  d. *a* and *b*

  e. *a, b,* and *c*

E 48. In addition to elevating body temperature and HR, exercising in the heat may increase which of the following?

  a. O$_2$ consumption beyond that expected for the activity

  b. muscle glycogen utilization

  c. lactate production

  d. general fatigue

  e. all of the above

X D 49. What occurs during an exercise bout in the heat?

A

  a. Q remains fairly constant.

  b. SV tends to increase.

  c. HR declines.

  d. *a* and *b*

  e. *a, b,* and *c*

C 50. Which of the following is true about nonshivering thermogenesis?

  a. It involves involuntary muscle contraction to increase metabolic heat during exercise in the cold.

  b. It causes peripheral vasoconstriction to limit heat transfer from the core to the periphery during an exercise bout in the cold.

  c. It occurs via stimulation of the sympathetic nervous system during cold weather activity.

  d. It facilitates loss of body heat during cold weather activity.

E 51. Which of the following is (are) true about hypothermia?

  a. It is the result of a high rate of heat loss to heat production.

  b. It can occur at a faster rate when the body is immersed in cold water.

c. It may occur more quickly during exercise in an environment that is cold, wet, and windy.

d. *a* and *b*

e. *a*, *b*, and *c*

52. Why do exercise and training become more difficult as one ascends to higher altitudes?

a. The partial pressure of O_2 decreases at altitude with a concomitant decrease in O_2 saturation.

b. $\dot{V}O_2$max decreases at altitude.

c. Respiratory alkalosis develops shortly after arrival at altitude.

d. *a* and *b*

e. *a*, *b*, and *c*

53. Which of the following pairs would be true during exercise at altitude?

a. decrease in barometric pressure–reduction of O_2 saturation

b. submaximal workload–higher HR

c. training at altitude–carry-over in training effect at sea level

d. *a* and *b*

e. *a*, *b*, and *c*

54. Why might women have an advantage over men when exposed to the cold?

a. lower sweat rate

b. smaller muscle mass

c. greater subcutaneous fat layer

d. *a* and *b*

e. *a*, *b*, and *c*

55. The hypoxic conditions of altitude result in which of the following physiological adjustments observed during an acute bout of exercise?

a. an increase in pulmonary ventilation

b. an increase in respiratory alkalosis

c. a loss of bicarbonate from the system

d. *a* and *b*

e. *a*, *b*, and *c*

56. The physiological effects of exercising in air pollution are dose related. What is (are) the major factor(s) determining dose?

a. volume of inhaled air

b. exposure time

c. concentration of the pollutants

d. *a* and *b*

e. *a*, *b*, and *c*

57. Which of the following pairs is (are) true regarding the physiological effects of air pollution?

a. sulfur dioxide–bronchoconstriction in asthmatics

b. carbon monoxide–decrease in O_2-carrying capacity

c. ozone–significant reduction in $\dot{V}O_2max$

d. *a* and *b*

e. *a*, *b*, and *c*

58. Humidity can affect the capacity to exercise in which of the following ways?

a. by decreasing the body's ability to evaporate sweat

b. by limiting the body's ability to lose heat

c. by limiting the effect of radiation as an avenue of heat loss

d. *a* and *b*

e. *a*, *b*, and *c*

59. Which of the following is true about overexercising?

a. It is a recommended way to increase training volume (e.g., swimming > 10,000 meters/day vs. < 5,000 meters/day) and has been found to elicit a faster physiological response in aerobic capacity.

b. It is a recommended way to increase training intensity (e.g., force on the muscle and/or stress on the cardiovascular system) and leads to faster improvement in conditioning response.

c. It is not recommended, but training intensities between 50 and 85 percent of $\dot{V}O_2$max are recommended to elicit the greatest improvement in aerobic response.

d. It is not recommended, but training at 90 percent $\dot{V}O_2$max coupled with high volume is advised for the quickest improvement in aerobic capacity.

60. Of the following, what is true about overtraining?

a. It occurs when one attempts to do more work than is physically tolerable.

b. It usually improves physical performance at a much faster rate compared to the established training regimen.

c. It results in anabolism proceeding at a faster rate than catabolism.

d. *a* and *b*

e. *a, b,* and *c*

61. The following observations were noted in an evaluation of a training program for a 21-year-old female cross-country runner: increased HR at a fixed workload, increased O_2 consumption at a fixed workload, and an increased incidence of illness during the training period. What might the coach conclude about this athlete from these observations and data?

a. She is overtraining.

b. She requires complete rest for three to five days.

c. She is not training up to her capacity.

d. *a* and *b*

e. *a, b,* and *c*

62. How can one prevent overuse injuries during a training regimen?

a. Avoid large increases in training volume.

b. Avoid large increases in training intensity.

   c. Increase training load by 10 percent (volume and intensity) per week.

   d. *a* and *b*

   e. *a*, *b*, and *c*

 63. To what is fatigue, as evidenced by a decrease in performance, theorized to be most likely due?

   a. failure of the fiber's contractile mechanism

   b. an imbalance in ATP requirement versus ATP delivery

   c. an increase in muscle acidity

   d. *a* and *b*

   e. *a*, *b*, and *c*

 64. Which of the following is (are) true regarding the process of glycolysis?

   a. It provides for the systematic degradation of glucose or glycogen to pyruvate.

   b. It is a predominant energy pathway during low-intensity, long-duration activity.

   c. It converts lactate to pyruvate in an anaerobic environment.

   d. *a* and *b*

   e. *a*, *b*, and *c*

65. The oxidative phosphorylation of glucose involves which of the following processes?

   a. glycolysis and electron transport chain

   b. Krebs cycle and beta oxidation

   c. glycolysis, Krebs cycle, and electron transport chain

   d. *a* and *b*

 66. Which of the statements below is (are) true regarding the interaction of exercise intensity, duration, and energy production during activity?

   a. In efforts of two to three minutes' duration, the anaerobic energy yield approximately equals the aerobic yield.

b. In prolonged endurance activities (>10 minutes), predominant energy-producing pathways involve anaerobic metabolism.

c. Most of the energy for performing a 400-meter dash would come from aerobic energy sources.

d. *a, b,* and *c*

67. Which of the following is (are) true about cardiac muscle, but *not* skeletal muscle?

a. Cardiac muscle contains branched, striated fibers with a single nucleus.

b. Cardiac muscle contains intercalated discs which connect the muscle cells to function as a unit.

c. Cardiac muscle cells can alter the force of contractions as a function of the degree of overlap between the actin and myosin filament.

d. *a* and *b*

e. *a, b,* and *c*

68. Which of the following pairs describes intercalated discs?

a. zonula occludens–tight junctions

b. zonular adherens–gap junctions

c. desmosomes–tight junctions

d. desmosomes–gap junctions

69. The four components of the cardiac induction system are listed below. Beginning with an impulse, what is the proper order of stimulation?

a. the SA node, the AV bundle (bundle of HIS), the AV node, the Purkinje fibers

b. the SA node, the Purkinje fibers, the AV bundle (bundle of HIS), the AV node

c. the SA node, the AV node, the AV bundle of HIS (AV bundle), the Purkinje fibers

d. the AV node, the SA node, the AV bundle (bundle of HIS), the Purkinje fibers

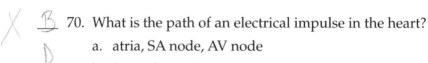

70. What is the path of an electrical impulse in the heart?

   a. atria, SA node, AV node

   b. SA node, Purkinje fiber, bundle of HIS

   c. AV node, atria, SA node

   d. SA node, atria, AV node

71. What name is given to the phenomenon of all cells becoming stimulated to contract when one heart cell is depolarized to contract?

   a. systole

   b. diastole

   c. functional syncytium

   d. intercalated disc electrical transference

72. A 21-year-old female who weighs 50 kilograms wishes to jump rope at 70 percent of her $\dot{V}O_2$max as a part of her fitness program. Her $\dot{V}O_2$max is 45 ml/kg/min. In METs and kilocalories, what is her total energy cost for 15 minutes of rope jumping?

   a. Working at 9 METs, her total energy cost would be 7.5 kcal/min or 112.5 kcal/15 min.

   b. Working at 12 METs, her total energy cost would be 150 kcal/15 min.

   c. Working at 9 METs, her total energy cost would be 450 kcal/15 min.

   d. *a* and *b*

   e. *a, b,* and *c*

73. For a 32-year-old, 70-kilogram male with a $\dot{V}O_2$max of 70 ml/kg/min, what would the energy cost be for cross-country skiing at 80 percent of his $\dot{V}O_2$max for 60 minutes?

   a. 16 METs–1,176 kcal/60 min

   b. 16 METs–1,470 kcal/60 min

   c. 20 METs–1,176 kcal/60 min

   d. 20 METs–1,470 kcal/60 min

___ 74. A physical therapist is working with a 70-year-old female who must now rely on a wheelchair for mobility after a leg injury. Will the elderly patient be able to push the wheelchair around at 50 percent of her $\dot{V}O_2$max for at least one minute before resting? Please note that (1) the patient's $\dot{V}O_2$max is 15 ml/kg/min, (2) her weight is 48 kilograms, and (3) wheelchair propulsion requires 2 METs.

 a. yes

 b. no

 c. not enough information given to determine an answer

_E_ 75. From a physiological perspective, which of the following scenarios would provide for a gain in an individual's health status?

 a. A sedentary person becomes moderately active.

 b. A person expends 200 kcal per activity session at least every other day.

 c. A person has achieved a high $\dot{V}O_2$max via exercise training.

 d. *a* and *b*

 e. *a*, *b*, and *c*

_D_ 76. What is accomplished by stretching before an exercise activity?

 a. increase in ROM of the joints

 b. decrease in resistance in muscles used in the activity

 c. decrease in the possibility of a hypotensive episode

 d. *a* and *b*

 e. *a*, *b*, and *c*

_E_ 77. Static stretching is a recommended technique to use in a flexibility program for which of the following reasons?

 a. There is less chance of injury.

 b. There is less muscle spindle activity.

 c. There is less DOMS.

 d. *a* and *b*

 e. *a*, *b*, and *c*

X C 78. Which of the following training adaptations might reduce
   D   the risk of CAD?
       a. a high plasma triglyceride concentration
       b. a lower high-density lipoprotein mass
       c. a decrease in lipoprotein lipase activity
       d. a decrease in hepatic lipase activity

D 79. Health-related and fitness benefits of muscular strength
       and endurance activities are based upon which of the
       following circumstances?
       a. improvement in abdominal strength and endurance
       b. increase in lower-back and hamstring flexibility
       c. prevention of low-back pain
       d. *a, b,* and *c*

X C 80. Which of the following health problems have been linked to
   B   obesity?
       a. diabetes
       b. binge-eating disorder
       c. hypertension
       d. asthma
       e. excessive wear on joints

X B 81. How does the physiological response to isometric exercise
   D   differ from that for isotonic exercise?
       a. It is anaerobic; time to muscular fatigue is proportional
          to percentage MVC; an MVC causes occlusion of arterial
          blood flow.
       b. It is primarily anaerobic; it involves a pressor response;
          time to muscular fatigue is proportional to percentage
          MVC.
       c. It involves the pressor response; contraction at 15 per-
          cent above MVC causes complete occlusion of arterial
          blood flow; pressor response involves no increase in
          $\dot{V}O_2$, HR, or Q.
       d. It is primarily anaerobic; pressor response involves a
          moderate increase in $\dot{V}O_2$, HR, and Q; there is no change
          in SV.

_B_ 82. How does the Valsalva maneuver significantly alter BP responses to isometric exercise?

    a. It increases intrathoracic pressure and increases venous return.

    b. It increases intrathoracic pressure and increases aortic BP.

    c. It causes external straining and increases venous return.

    d. It increases aortic BP and increases ventricular wall volume loading.

X _C_ 83. Immediately after isometric exercise, which of the following scenario(s) will occur?

B

    a. a decrease in BP, a decrease in baroreceptor activity, an increase in HR

    b. an increase in BP, an increase in venous return, an increase in systemic vascular resistance

    c. an increase in venous return, a decrease in systemic vascular resistance, a decrease in BP

    d. *a* and *b*

    e. *a, b,* and *c*

X _B_ 84. Which of the following is (are) true with regard to specificity and fitness?

E

    a. Training effect is limited to the muscle fibers involved in the activity.

    b. Muscle fiber adapts specifically to a type of activity.

    c. Mitochondria demonstrate greater adaptation with endurance activity.

    d. *a* and *b*

    e. *a, b,* and *c*

X _B_ 85. Which of the following list of increases best demonstrates the aerobic system?

D

    a. key glycolytic enzymes; all-out exercise performance; mitochondrial size and number

    b. key glycolytic enzymes; capillaries of the trained muscle; mitochondrial size and number

    c. aerobic enzymes; capillaries; resting level of anaerobic substrates

    d. aerobic enzymes; oxidation of CHO; mitochondrial size and number

86. The specificity of weight training is associated with which of the following training components matched with expected program results?

    a. training with force against high resistance; a small number of repetitions; gains in muscle strength demonstrated

    b. training with force against high resistance; a small number of repetitions; gains in muscle size demonstrated

    c. training with force against low resistance; high number of repetitions; gains in muscular endurance demonstrated

    d. *a* and *b*

    e. *a, b,* and *c*

87. Which test(s) is (are) specific to the selected sport activity?

    a. GXT on a treadmill–running

    b. exercise test in a swim flume or a pool with a tether–swimming

    c. GXT on an arm ergometer–bicycling

    d. *a* and *b*

    e. *a, b,* and *c*

88. In a GXT, what is the term for the power output or rate of O_2 uptake at which ventilation departs from linearity?

    a. ventilatory threshold–T_{vent}

    b. ventilatory threshold–OBLA

    c. onset of blood lactate–T_{vent}

    d. onset of blood lactate–OBLA

89. Which of the following is (are) true of what is most often termed the anaerobic threshold?

    a. With aerobic training, fat metabolism is enhanced; T_{vent} shifts to the right.

b. The ratio $VE/\dot{V}O_2$ can be a good estimate of the OBLA or T_{vent}.

c. Determination of T_{vent} is a good indicator of endurance performance.

d. *a* and *b*

e. *a*, *b*, and *c*

90. Which of the following three major physiological factors affect cardiorespiratory endurance performance?

a. $\dot{V}O_2$max; number of slow twitch-oxidative (SO) (type I) muscle fibers; exercise O_2 economy

b. $\dot{V}O_2$max; OBLA; exercise O_2 economy

c. $\dot{V}O_2$max; anaerobic threshold; number of fast twitch-glycolytic (FG) (type IIa) muscle fibers

d. *a* and *b*

e. *a*, *b*, and *c*

91. With 84 days of detraining, which of the following would be observed?

a. a decrease in $\dot{V}O_2$max; a decrease in a-vO_2 diff max; a decrease in capillary number

b. a decrease in Q max; a decrease in HR max; capillary number unchanged

c. a decrease in a-vO_2 diff max; a decrease in number of mitochondria; Q unchanged

d. a decrease in capillaries; an increase in HR max; a decrease in $\dot{V}O_2$max

92. What is a common-sense guideline to follow to prevent training-induced injuries as a result of overtraining?

a. Follow the "10 percent rule."

b. Train by not increasing the intensity or duration of a session by more than 10 percent.

c. Increase weekly mileage by 5 miles/week for a 50 mile/week runner.

d. *a* and *b*

e. *a*, *b*, and *c*

E 93. Which of the following are observable signs associated with overtraining?

   a. an increase in HR; a decrease in performance; an increase in injury rate

   b. a decrease in appetite; a disturbance in sleep pattern; postural hypotension

   c. an increase in resting BP; an increase in episodes of illness; weight loss

   d. *a* and *b*

   e. *a*, *b*, and *c*

E 94. Human skeletal muscle can be divided into what three fiber classifications?

   a. slow twitch, fast twitch, intermediate

   b. slow twitch-oxidative (SO), fast twitch-oxidative-glycolytic (FOG), fast twitch-glycolytic (FG)

   c. type I, type IIa, type IIb

   d. *a* and *b*

   e. *a*, *b*, and *c*

A 95. Of the following, which matches the skeletal muscle fiber type to its functional characteristic?

   a. type I–slow oxidative; low force production, fatigue resistant

   b. type IIa–slow oxidative; low force production, fatigable

   c. type IIb–fast-oxidative glycolytic; high force production, fatigue resistant

   d. intermediate–fast glycolytic; high force production, fatigable

L 96. Choose the pair(s) in which the characteristic of the fiber type matches the fiber nomenclature.

D

   a. oxidative metabolism–SO

   b. slow maximal shortening velocity–type I

   c. low activity of myosin-ATPase–type IIB

   d. *a* and *b*

   e. *a*, *b*, and *c*

X B 97. In the sliding filament theory of muscle contraction, actin-myosin interaction is facilitated by what two mechanisms?

A

   a. the release of Ca^{++} from the sarcoplasmic reticulum; the presence of ATP

   b. the attachment of ATP to troponin; myosin activation

   c. action potential initiation; the presence of ATP

   d. the release of Ca^{++} from the sarcoplasmic reticulum; the propagation of the impulse through the T tubule

X D 98. During the "recharging" phase in the sliding filament theory, the following events occur. What is the correct sequence of events?

C

   a. The muscle returns to resting state, Ca^{++} is sequestered, actomyosin decouples, actin and myosin are recycled, ATP is resynthesized, and the nerve impulse ceases.

   b. Ca^{++} is sequestered, actin and myosin are recycled, acto-myosin decouples, ATP is resynthesized, the nerve impulse ceases, and the muscle returns to resting state.

   c. ATP is resynthesized, actomyosin decouples, actin and myosin are recycled, the nerve impulse ceases, Ca^{++} is sequestered, and the muscle returns to resting state.

   d. ATP is resynthesized, actomyosin decouples, the nerve impulse ceases, actin and myosin are recycled, Ca^{++} is sequestered, and the muscle returns to resting state.

C 99. Normal body movements involve sustained contractions and do *not* involve single muscle twitches. What is the term for normal body movements involving the addition of successive twitches; and if the frequency of stimuli is increased further, what is this called?

   a. a submaximal response–a maximal response

   b. summation–tonus

   c. summation–tetanus

   d. tonus–tetanus

E 100. What is true about the overload principle?

   a. It requires a progressive increase in the intensity of a workout over the course of training as fitness capacity improves.

b. It describes a condition in which a tissue or organ is caused to work against a load that it is not accustomed to.

c. It describes the need to increase the load in exercise to cause further adaptation of a system.

d. *a* and *b*

e. *a*, *b*, and *c*

101. Muscle adaptations as a result of training are due to what?

a. the principle of specificity

b. PRE

c. the principle of overload

d. *a* and *b*

e. *a*, *b*, and *c*

102. With regard to strength training and the development of muscular fitness, why is recovery time important between sets and sessions?

a. to replenish energy stores; to minimize injury

b. to decrease muscle soreness; to maintain metabolic balance

c. to resynthesize ATP; to decrease overall discomfort

d. *a* and *b*

e. *a*, *b*, and *c*

103. What is the number of repetitions and sets recommended to predominantly increase muscle strength?

a. 1-5 repetitions; four sets

b. 6-12 repetitions; three sets

c. 20 repetitions; two sets

d. 3 repetitions; five sets

104. Which of the following are true with regard to strength training?

a. When repetitions are low (e.g., 3-5), greater strength is developed; four to eight sets are optimal for strength; rest periods should be two to four minutes in length.

  b. When repetitions are high (e.g., 15-25), muscle endur-
     ance is developed; two to four sets are optimal; rest
     periods should be 30 to 90 seconds in length.

  c. 8-12 RM performed during one set will provide im-
     provement in strength similar to that seen with a
     "multiple-set system."

  d. *a* and *b*

  e. *a, b,* and *c*

105. Choose the pair(s) in which the abnormal condition is
     matched with the appropriate normal symptom.

  a. dyspnea–12 breaths per minute at rest

  b. orthostatic hypotension–120/80 mm Hg

  c. PVC–bradycardia

  d. *a* and *b*

  e. *a, b,* and *c*

106. During low-intensity exercise (e.g., jogging) what happens
     to SBP and DBP, respectively?

  a. increase–very little change

  b. increase–increase

  c. decrease–very little change

  d. decrease–decrease

107. Static exercise or activities that involve high resistances
     cause what changes in SBP and DBP, respectively?

  a. increase–very little change

  b. increase–increase

  c. decrease–very little change

  d. decrease–decrease

108. Body inversion techniques used to facilitate a strength-
     training response or relieve low-back pain cause what
     changes in SBP and DBP, respectively?

  a. increase–decrease

  b. increase–increase

  c. decrease–no change

  d. decrease–decrease

E 109. Which of the following is (are) indicative of a hypertensive BP response?

   a. BP > 140/90 mm Hg; current use of antihypertensive medication
   b. increased total peripheral resistance; elevated Q
   c. exercise BP of > 225/90 mm Hg
   d. *a* and *b*
   e. *a, b,* and *c*

D 110. Which of the following is (are) true about hypotension?

   a. It is a restricted BP response pattern.
   b. It is often noted in individuals with severe ischemic heart disease.
   c. It is demonstrated as an inadequate rise in SBP (<20 mm Hg increase from rest).
   d. *a, b,* and *c*

D 111. Which of the following changes in skeletal muscle results from anaerobic training?

   a. a decrease in the capacity of the phosphagen system
   b. a decrease in the muscular stores of ATP and PC
   c. a slower ATP turnover rate
   d. increase in glycolytic enzyme activities

C 112. What changes at rest are induced by training?

   a. increased size of the left atrial cavity in endurance athletes
   b. decrease in left ventricular wall thickness in non-endurance athletes
   c. decrease in the intrinsic atrial HR in endurance athletes
   d. decrease in parasympathetic tone

A 113. What changes occurring during maximal work are influenced by training?

   a. increase in $\dot{V}O_2max$; increase in Q max
   b. increase in HR max; increase in SV max

    c. increase in sympathetic drive; increase in intrinsic pace-maker rate

    d. decrease in lactate production; decrease in blood flow per kilogram of active muscle

__A__ 114. What cause Q to increase during exercise?

    a. a rise in HR; an increase in SV

    b. a rise in BP; an increase in peripheral resistance

    c. a rise in HR; an increase in venous return

    d. an increase in SV; a decrease in parasympathetic tone

__D__ 115. What terms are given to the movement of gas in and out of the lung and the volume of air inhaled or exhaled in a single breath, respectively?

    a. total lung capacity–ventilation

    b. alveolar air–tidal volume

    c. inspired volume–ventilation

    d. ventilation–tidal volume

__D__ 116. Exercise training can benefit type I diabetics in which of the following ways?

    B

    a. lowering body fat

    b. increasing peripheral sensitivity to insulin

    c. increasing glucose intolerance

    d. *a* and *b*

    e. *a*, *b*, and *c*

REFERENCES FOR FURTHER STUDY

1. ACSM. (1991). *Guidelines for exercise testing and prescription* (4th ed.). Malvern, PA: Lea & Febiger.

2. ACSM. (1993). *ACSM's resource manual for guidelines for exercise testing and prescription* (2nd ed.). Malvern, PA: Lea & Febiger.

3. ACSM. (1995). *ACSM's guidelines for exercise testing and prescription* (5th ed.). Baltimore: Williams & Wilkins.

4. Anderson, K.N. (Ed.). (1994). *Mosby's medical, nursing, and allied health dictionary* (4th ed.). St. Louis: Mosby.

5. Baumgartner, T., & Jackson, A. (1995). *Measurement for evaluation in physical education and exercise science*. Madison, WI: Brown & Benchmark.

6. Fox, E., Bowers, R., & Foss, M. (1993). *The physiological basis for exercise and sport* (5th ed.). Madison, WI: Brown & Benchmark.

7. Howley, E.T., & Franks, B.D. (1997). *Health fitness instructor's handbook* (3rd ed.). Champaign, IL: Human Kinetics.

8. McArdle, W.D., Katch, F.I., & Katch, V.I. (1991). *Exercise physiology: Energy, nutrition, and human performance* (3rd ed.). Malvern, PA: Lea & Febiger.

9. Nieman, D.C. (1995). *Fitness and sports medicine: A health-related approach* (3rd ed.). Palo Alto, CA: Bull.

10. Powers, S.K., & Howley, E.T. (1997). *Exercise physiology: Theory and applications to fitness and performance* (3rd ed.). Madison, WI: Brown & Benchmark.

11. Wilmore, J.H., & Costill, D.L. (1994). *Physiology of sport and exercise*. Champaign, IL: Human Kinetics.

ANSWERS

Question number	Answer	KSA number	Reference	Page number
1	b	1	7	51
2	a	1	10	33, 46
3	a	2	10	41
4	c	2	10	49
5	d	3	7	66
			10	160
6	b	3	10	46
7	d	3	2	572
8	a	3	2	70
9	b	3	2	70
10	e	3	10	272
11	e	3	4	1524
12	d	3	4	216
13	e	3	4	1035
14	a	3	4	87
15	a	4	7	51

Question number	Answer	KSA number	Reference	Page number
			10	56
16	d	5	3	158, 166
17	d	5	10	294
18	c	5	10	402
19	e	5	7	166, 179
			3	59
20	c	6	5	246
21	d	7	10	165
22	d	7	10	46, 50
23	c	7	7	73
24	d	7	2	82
			7	74
25	e	7	10	47
26	d	8	2	87
27	a	8	6	387-389
28	e	8	7	72
29	d	9	10	398
30	e	9	10	398
31	d	9	10	246
32	d	9	11	70
33	e	9	11	71
34	a	9	2	103
35	b	9	10	246, 398
36	e	10	7	129
37	d	10	3	166
38	e	10	2	572
39	d	11	7	215
40	b	11	7	215

Question number	Answer	KSA number	Reference	Page number
41	d	11	10	271
42	e	12	2	383
43	e	12	10	471
44	e	12	10	290
45	b	12	9	207
46	e	12	9	221
47	e	13	9	521
			10	450
			11	248
48	e	13	11	250
49	a	13	11	252
50	c	13	11	261
51	e	13	10	451
52	e	13	2	139
53	d	13	10	442
54	c	13	11	463
55	e	13	11	270
56	e	13	7	286
57	e	13	7	286
58	d	13	11	244
59	c	14	3	158
60	a	14	11	303
61	d	14	11	304
62	e	14	10	397
63	e	15	10	362
			11	114
64	a	16	11	96
			10	29

Question number	Answer	KSA number	Reference	Page number
65	c	16	10	33
66	a	16	2	61
			7	52
67	d	17	10	153
68	d	17	11	166
69	c	17	11	166
70	d	17	11	166
71	c	17	10	154
72	a	19	7	128
73	a	19	7	128
74	a	19	7	128
			11	523
75	e	19	7	222
76	d	20	1	185
			10	290
77	e	20	10	402
78	d	20	9	342
79	d	20	9	32, 151
			7	11
80	b	20	7	194
81	d	21	1	31
82	b	21	1	32
83	b	21	1	32
84	e	22	2	82
			10	230
85	d	22	2	82
			8	429
86	e	22	3	173

Question number	Answer	KSA number	Reference	Page number
			10	247
87	d	22	2	89
88	a	23	1	17
89	e	23	7	64
			9	181
90	d	23	9	194
91	c	24	7	71
92	e	25	10	397
93	e	25	9	512
94	e	27	10	135
95	a	27	7	55
96	d	27	2	98
97	a	28	2	94
98	c	28	6	101
99	c	29	10	144
100	e	30	7	293
			6	170
101	e	30	9	224
102	e	31	2	338
103	a	31	7	306
			10	399
104	d	31	7	306
105	d	32	2	67
			10	268
106	a	33	2	70
			9	177
			8	302

Question number	Answer	KSA number	Reference	Page number
107	b	33	2	70
			7	73
			8	302
108	b	33	8	305
109	e	34	3	206
			2	188
110	d	34	1	74
111	d	35	6	327
112	c	35	6	327
113	a	35	6	341
114	a	36	6	252
			10	160
115	d	36	6	204
			10	184
116	b	37	2	191

CHAPTER 6

Human Development and Aging

© Terry Wild Studio

Of the 10 ACSM KSA categories, the least comprehensive is Human Development and Aging, the topic of this chapter. In fact, on the basis of previous ACSM Health/Fitness Instructor certification examinations, it is likely that you will receive only three questions from this category. Emphasis is placed on your ability to distinguish differences between young children and older adults relative to unique adaptations to exercise, differences in exercise prescription, and the developmental effects of aging on physiological fitness.

PRACTICE QUESTIONS

Directions: Each question is followed by either four or five possible answers. Select the *best* answer to the question.

1. Children are less able than adults to thermoregulate during heat exposure because children exhibit which of the following characteristics?

   a. lower threshold for the onset of sweating, lower skin blood flow, higher sweat output from heat-activated sweat glands, and smaller surface area to body mass ratio

   b. lower threshold for the onset of sweating, higher skin blood flow, lower sweat output from heat-activated sweat glands, and smaller surface area to body mass ratio

   c. higher threshold for the onset of sweating, lower skin blood flow, lower sweat output from heat-activated sweat glands, and larger surface area to body mass ratio

   d. higher threshold for the onset of sweating, higher skin blood flow, higher sweat output from heat-activated sweat glands, and larger surface area to body mass ratio

2. At what rate do women over the age of 35 tend to lose bone mass?

   a. .05 percent per year

   b. 1.0 percent per year

   c. 1.5 percent per year

   d. 2.0 percent per year

C 3. Within an elderly population, what change occurs in resting HR?

   a. decrease

   b. increase

   c. little to no change

   d. increase in men but decrease in women

   e. increase in women but decrease in men

A 4. As people age, what change occurs in maximal HR?

   a. decrease

   b. increase

   c. little to no change

   d. increase in men but decrease in women

   e. increase in women but decrease in men

XB
C 5. Peak flexibility, as measured by the sit-and-reach test, is generally obtained at what age?

   a. prior to 10 years of age

   b. between 12 and 15 years of age

   c. during the late teens and early 20s

   d. between 30 and 35 years of age

D 6. By 65 years of age, what is the approximate decline in muscular strength?

   a. 5 percent

   b. 10 percent

   c. 15 percent

   d. 20 percent

B 7. $\dot{V}O_2$max in adulthood declines at about what rate per year?

   a. 0.5 percent

   b. 1.0 percent

   c. 1.5 percent

   d. 2.0 percent

X

___D___ 8. Excessive endurance exercise in a prepubescent child could place the child at increased risk for what problem?

   a. a decrease in height
   b. an epiphyseal growth plate injury
   c. rotator cuff injury
   d. none

X ___C___ 9. What is the minimum stage or age a child should reach before being permitted to perform maximum lifts (1RM)?

   a. 10 years of age
   b. 18 years of age
   c. Tanner stage 3 level of maturity
   d. Tanner stage 5 level of maturity

___E___ 10. What is true about elderly individuals who regularly participate in a resistance-training program?

   a. Significant increases occur in muscle cross-sectional area within the first six weeks of training.
   b. They tend to be more self-sufficient.
   c. They tend to perform daily living skills with greater ease.
   d. They show no physiological advantage over peers who maintain a sedentary lifestyle.
   e. b and c

___E___ 11. The exercise leader should be aware of leadership techniques that meet the needs of special populations. Which of the following pertain(s) especially to young children from special populations engaged in an exercise program?

   a. frequent change of activity
   b. frequent rest periods
   c. frequent use of demonstrations
   d. a and b
   e. a, b, and c

_C_ 12. At maximal intensities, how much lower is the cardiac output of older adults than that of younger individuals?

    a. 1-5 percent

    b. 10-20 percent

    c. 20-30 percent

    d. 30-40 percent

X _A_ 13. What change occurs in residual volume by 70 years of age?
_D_

    a. It decreases by 5-10 percent.

    b. It decreases by 30-50 percent.

    c. It increases by 5-10 percent.

    d. It increases by 30-50 percent.

X _D_ 14. Which of the following decrease(s) with age?
_E_

    a. size of muscle fibers

    b. number of muscle fibers

    c. maximal HR

    d. *a* and *c*

    e. *a, b,* and *c*

X _A_ 15. ACSM guidelines recommend for young healthy individu-
_C_ als an exercise intensity that is between 50 and 85 percent of HRR. What is the recommended percentage for older adults?

    a. 50-60 percent of HRR

    b. 50-60 percent of HR max

    c. 50-70 percent of HRR

    d. 50-70 percent of HR max

X _E_ 16. In comparison to the ACSM guideline recommending that
_C_ young children perform resistance-training exercise no more than two days per week, what is recommended for elderly individuals?

    a. daily

    b. one day per week

c. two days per week

d. three days per week

e. five days per week

A 17. What increase, if any, is demonstrated by older adults who participate regularly in a strength-training program?

a. increased strength in the absence of muscle hypertrophy

b. increased strength with moderate muscle hypertrophy

c. increased strength with significant muscle hypertrophy

d. little to no increase in muscle strength

A 18. What increase, if any, is generally demonstrated in pre-pubescent children who regularly participate in a weight-training program?

a. increased strength in the absence of muscle hypertrophy

b. increased strength with moderate muscle hypertrophy

c. increased strength with significant muscle hypertrophy

d. little to no increase in muscular strength

C 19. What is the most appropriate exercise modification for an elderly individual with degenerative joint disease?

a. bench stepping

b. stair climbing

c. stationary cycling

d. running

C 20. What is the most appropriate exercise modification for an elderly individual with hypertension?

a. emphasis on high-resistance, low-repetition, isotonic training

b. emphasis on high-resistance, high-repetition, isotonic training

c. emphasis on low-resistance, low-repetition, isotonic training

d. emphasis on isometric training

E 21. What adjustment should be made by the elderly individual who is engaged in resistance training during periods of arthritic pain?

    a. Reduce training from two days per week to one day per week.

    b. Reduce training from three days per week to two days per week.

    c. Reduce exercise intensity and increase the number of repetitions.

    d. Reduce both exercise intensity and number of repetitions.

    e. Avoid resistance training during periods of pain.

REFERENCES FOR FURTHER STUDY

1. ACSM. (1993). *ACSM's resource manual for guidelines for exercise testing and prescription* (2nd ed.). Malvern, PA: Lea & Febiger.

2. ACSM. (1995). *ACSM's guidelines for exercise testing and prescription* (5th ed.). Baltimore: Williams & Wilkins.

3. Payne, V.G., & Isaacs, L.D. (1995). *Human motor development: A lifespan approach* (3rd ed.). Mountain View, CA: Mayfield.

ANSWERS

Question number	Answer	KSA number	Reference	Page number
1	c	1	2	224
2	b	1	1	420
3	c	1	2	228
4	a	1	2	228
5	c	1	3	161
6	d	1	1	420
7	b	1	3	153

Question number	Answer	KSA number	Reference	Page number
8	b	2	2	224
9	d	2	3	158
10	e	3	2	231
11	e	4	1	325
12	c	5	1	418
13	d	5	1	419
14	e	5	3	161
15	c	6	2	231
16	c	6	2	233
17	a	7	1	420
18	a	7	3	160
19	c	8	1	423
20	c	8	1	423
21	e	8	2	233

CHAPTER 7

Pathophysiology and Risk Factors

© Photophile/L.L.T. Rhodes

We suggest that you begin your study of this ACSM KSA category, titled Pathophysiology and Risk Factors, by first memorizing the CAD risk factors listed on page 18 of *ACSM's Guidelines for Exercise Testing and Prescription* (ACSM, 1995). Of the approximately six questions that you are likely to encounter from this category, one or two will deal specifically with the identification of common medications (see ACSM, 1995; appendix A).

PRACTICE QUESTIONS

Directions: Each question is followed by either four or five possible answers. Select the *best* answer to the question.

 1. What change in cholesterol is associated with an increase in physical activity?

   a. an increase in LDL-C

   b. an increase in HDL-C

   c. an increase in both HDL-C and LDL-C

   d. a decrease in both HDL-C and LDL-C

 2. A reduction in dietary sodium intake, weight reduction, and an increase in physical activity will generally allow a patient to modify which of the following CAD risk factors?

   a. hypercholesterolemia

   b. hypertension

   c. diabetes mellitus

   d. VLDL-C

 3. Of the following cholesterol measures, which is the best determinant of CAD risk?

   a. TC:HDL-C ratio

   b. HDL-C:LDL-C ratio

   c. TC

   d. LDL-C:VLDL-C ratio

B 4. In the mild (stage 1) hypertensive, what would be the expected range for adult resting SBP and DBP, respectively?

   a. 130-139 mm Hg; 85-90 mm Hg

   b. 140-159 mm Hg; 90-99 mm Hg

   c. 160-179 mm Hg; 100-109 mm Hg

   d. 180-209 mm Hg; 110-119 mm Hg

C 5. In the moderate (stage 2) hypertensive, what would be the expected range of adult resting SBP and DBP, respectively?

   a. 130-139 mm Hg; 85-90 mm Hg

   b. 140-159 mm Hg; 90-99 mm Hg

   c. 160-179 mm Hg; 100-109 mm Hg

   d. 180-209 mm Hg; 110-119 mm Hg

A 6. What procedure should be followed when SBP and DBP fall into different classification categories?

   a. Classify according to the higher category.

   b. Classify according to the lower category.

   c. Do not classify at this time, but continue to retest weekly until both SBP and DBP measures fall within the same category.

   d. Do not classify at this time, but continue to retest every six weeks until both SBP and DBP measures fall within the same category.

X B 7. Which of the following, if any, is (are) true regarding hypertension?

   a. Hypertension is more prevalent among women and blacks than among men and whites.

   b. Primary hypertension is caused by identifiable endocrine or structural disorders.

   c. One is hypertensive if exercise BP > 140/90 mm Hg.

   d. All of the above are true statements.

   e. None of the above are true statements.

X D 8. What lipoprotein is the primary carrier of serum choles-
   B   terol?

      a. HDL-C

      b. LDL-C

      c. VLDL-C

      d. triglyceride

C 9. What lipoprotein is primarily responsible for transporting
      cholesterol out of the system?

      a. VLDL-C

      b. LDL-C

      c. HDL-C

      d. triglyceride

E 10. What causes anemia?

      a. decrease in red blood cell production

      b. increase in red blood cell production

      c. increase in red blood cell destruction

      d. blood loss

      e. *a, c,* and *d*

C 11. Which of the following is the most desirable TC:HDL-C
      ratio?

      a. TC 199:HDL-C 38

      b. TC 190:HDL-C 50

      c. TC 210:HDL-C 62

      d. TC 175:HDL-C 36

E 12. What can result from a mismatch between active muscle O_2
      supply and demand?

      a. ischemic pain

      b. claudication

      c. tightness or cramping

      d. *a* and *b*

      e. *a, b,* and *c*

X B 13. Given the following health information, which abnormal
D   findings for a 34-year-old male would require consultation
with a physician or allied health professional prior to grant-
ing exercise clearance? Resting BP 130/96; resting HR
72 beats per minute; TC 210; LDL-C 155 mg/dl; HDL-C
38 mg/dl

    a. BP, TC, and HDL-C are too high.

    b. BP, TC, and LDL-C are too high while HDL-C is too low.

    c. BP, TC, LDL-C are too low while HDL-C is too high.

    d. BP, TC, and LDL-C are too high.

D 14. What should the exercise professional recommend to a
client who indicates a desire to increase exercise intensity
because he believes his sudden breathlessness during mild
exertion is a matter of not pushing himself hard enough?

    a. Increase the exercise intensity by 5 percent.

    b. Increase the exercise duration from 30 to 45 minutes but
maintain the current level of exercise intensity.

    c. Decrease the exercise duration from 30 to 15 minutes
and increase exercise intensity by 20 percent.

    d. Require the client to consult with his physician before
proceeding with any exercise program.

D 15. What symptom(s) is (are) associated with asthma?

    a. wheezing

    b. nonproductive cough

    c. productive cough in which sputum is produced

    d. *a* and *b*

    e. *a* and *c*

E 16. What symptom(s) is (are) associated with bronchitis?

    a. wheezing

    b. nonproductive cough

    c. productive cough in which sputum is produced

    d. *a* and *b*

    e. *a* and *c*

17. With exercise-induced asthma, when will the onset of the attack generally occur?

   a. 5-15 minutes following exercise

   b. 4-6 hours following exercise

   c. 12-18 hours following exercise

   d. *a* and *b*

   e. *a* and *c*

18. Is there a need for a male with the following preexercise test evaluation to consult with a medical professional before participating in a physical activity program? 20 years of age; weight 62 kilograms; hemoglobin 14 g/dl; fasting glucose 205 mg/dl; HDL-C 42 mg/dl; LDL-C 120 mg/dl; SBP 138 mm Hg; DBP 83 mm Hg

   a. No, all values are within appropriate ranges.

   b. Yes, HDL-C is too low.

   c. Yes, fasting glucose is too high.

   d. Yes, there are signs of anemia.

   e. *c* and *d*

19. What should the exercise professional do with regard to a client who wishes to begin a jogging program geared to strengthening the muscles in his painful lower back?

   a. Have the client perform the Cooper 1.5-mile run before recommending a specific exercise program.

   b. Instruct the client to run only on a soft indoor track.

   c. Show the client how to do back hyperextension exercises in order to strengthen the lower back before starting a jogging program.

   d. Require the client to consult his personal physician before starting an exercise program.

   e. Instruct the client to engage in bed rest for three weeks before starting a jogging program.

20. Which of the following known muscular adaptions will persist, even in the face of detraining, in individuals

who have participated in intense exercise for many years?

a. muscle fiber size

b. mitochondrial density

c. mitochondrial enzyme activity

d. muscle capillarization

e. *b* and *c*

 21. What is associated with detraining?

a. a decrease in muscle fiber size

b. an increase in mitochondrial density

c. a decrease in mitochondrial enzyme activity

d. *a* and *b*

e. *a* and *c*

22. What is the term for an injury caused by the overstretching or tearing of a muscle or tendon?

a. sprain

b. strain

c. subluxation

d. bruise

 23. What is the term for an injury caused by the overstretching or tearing of ligamentous tissue?

a. sprain

b. strain

c. subluxation

d. bruise

 24. What is the term for an inflammatory disorder affecting the sac lying between muscle and bone?

a. bursitis

b. tendinitis

c. plantar fascitis

d. myositis

B 25. What is the term for an inflammatory disorder of muscles and/or tendons that attach at the elbow joint?

a. capsulitis

b. epicondylitis

c. bursitis

d. synovitis

D 26. What is the term for an inflammatory disorder of the fibrous tissue that attaches muscle to bone?

a. bursitis

b. capsulitis

c. synovitis

d. tendinitis

C 27. Which of the following is the definition of osteoporosis?

a. an inflammatory disease of the joints that affects only older adults

b. an inflammatory disease of the joints that can affect the young and old alike

c. a loss of bone mass resulting in bone thinning and bone weakening

d. a loss of serotonin

A 28. What is the term for an inflammatory joint condition with an underlying autoimmune component?

a. osteoarthritis

b. osteoporosis

c. chondromalacia

d. rheumatoid arthritis

e. a and d

A 29. Which of the following refers to the softening of cartilage?

a. chondromalacia

b. osteoporosis

c. tendinitis

d. cardiomyopathy

30. Which of the following factors is (are) believed to contribute to coronary artery injury?

a. hypercholesterolemia

b. hypertension

c. viral infections

d. *a* and *b*

e. *a, b,* and *c*

 31. How does exercise influence the atherosclerotic process?

a. It decreases HDL-C, increases LDL-C, and decreases BP.

b. It increases HDL-C, increases LDL-C, and decreases BP.

c. It increases HDL-C, decreases LDL-C, and increases BP.

d. It increases HDL-C, decreases LDL-C, and decreases BP.

 32. Which of the following is a nitrate or nitroglycerin?

a. isosorbide dinitrate (Isordil)

b. nifedipine (Procardia)

c. bumetanide (Bumex)

d. propranolol (Inderal)

 33. Which of the following is (are) antianginal calcium channel blocker(s)?

a. propranolol (Inderal)

b. nifedipine (Procardia)

c. diltiazem (Cardizem)

d. *a* and *b*

e. *b* and *c*

 34. Which of the following is an antianginal beta blocker?

a. furosemide (Lasix)

b. metoprolol (Lopressor)

c. ephedrine (Adrenalin)

d. quinidine (Quinidex)

35. Which of the following is a diuretic?
    a. furosemide (Lasix)
    b. captopril (Capoten)
    c. quinapril (Accupril)
    d. diltiazem (Cardizem)

36. Which of the following is known as an angiotensin-converting enzyme inhibitor?
    a. propranolol (Inderal)
    b. metoprolol (Lopressor)
    c. furosemide (Lasix)
    d. captopril (Capoten)

37. Which of the following is a peripheral vasodilator?
    a. acebutolol (Sectral)
    b. hydralazine (Apresoline)
    c. metoprolol (Lopressor)
    d. prazosin (Minipress)

38. Which of the following selections, if any, is (are) an anti-arrhythmic medication(s)?
    a. quinidine (Quinidex)
    b. tocainide (Tonocard)
    c. encainide (Enkaid)
    d. a, b, and c
    e. none of the above

39. Which of the following, if any, is (are) bronchodilator(s)?
    a. albuterol (Ventolin)
    b. theophylline (Theo-Dur)
    c. a and b
    d. none of the above

_C_ 40. How may the ingestion of nicotine influence one's response to exercise?

   a. by increasing both SBP and DBP, decreasing HR, and increasing pulse pressure

   b. by increasing SBP, decreasing DBP, increasing HR, and decreasing pulse pressure

   c. by increasing SBP, DBP, HR, and pulse pressure

   d. by increasing SBP, decreasing DBP, increasing HR, and increasing pulse pressure

X _B_ 41. How may the ingestion of an antihistamine influence one's response to exercise?

   D a. no effect on BP but an increase in HR and exercise capacity

   b. no effect on HR but an increase in BP and exercise capacity

   c. no effect on HR or BP but an increase in exercise capacity

   d. no effect on HR, BP, ECG, or exercise capacity

X _D_ 42. What effect does the ingestion of alcohol have on one's response to exercise?

   B a. It increases exercise capacity.

   b. It may provoke arrhythmias.

   c. It decreases HR.

   d. It decreases both HR and BP.

X _D_ 43. How may the ingestion of caffeine influence one's response to exercise?

   E a. It may provoke arrhythmias.

   b. It may provoke increase in HR and BP in a caffeine-naive user.

   c. It provokes little to no change in HR or BP in the frequent caffeine user.

   d. b and c

   e. a, b, c, and d

_A_ 44. How may the ingestion of diet pills containing sympatho-mimetic amines influence one's response to exercise?

   a. It increases HR and BP.

   b. It increases HR but decreases BP.

   c. It significantly improves sprinting speed.

   d. *a* and *c*

   e. *b* and *c*

_C_ 45. What is the influence of ingesting minor tranquilizers on one's response to exercise?

   a. no significant effect on HR, BP, or exercise capacity except for the side benefit of controlling anxiety

   b. no significant effect on HR or BP except for the side benefit of controlling anxiety and increasing exercise capacity

   c. increase in HR, BP, and exercise capacity

   d. increase in HR and BP but decrease in exercise capacity

REFERENCES FOR FURTHER STUDY

1. ACSM. (1993). *ACSM's resource manual for guidelines for exercise testing and prescription* (2nd ed.). Malvern, PA: Lea & Febiger.

2. ACSM. (1995). *ACSM's guidelines for exercise testing and prescription* (5th ed.). Baltimore: Williams & Wilkins.

3. Anderson, K.N. (Ed.). (1994). *Mosby's medical, nursing, and allied health dictionary* (4th ed.). St. Louis: Mosby.

4. Baechle, T.R. (Ed.). (1994). *Essentials of strength training and conditioning.* Champaign, IL: Human Kinetics.

5. Howley, E.T., & Franks, B.D. (1997). *Health fitness instructor's handbook* (3rd ed.). Champaign, IL: Human Kinetics.

ANSWERS

Question number	Answer	KSA number	Reference	Page number
1	b	1	1	158
2	b	1	2	207
3	a	1	5	42
			4	219
4	b	2	2	33
5	c	2	2	33
6	a	2	2	33
7	e	2	2	206
8	b	2	1	152
9	c	2	1	153
10	e	2	3	84
11	c	3	5	42
12	e	4	2	209
13	d	4	2	36
14	d	5	1	221
15	d	5	1	193
16	e	5	1	193
17	d	5	5	365
18	c	6	2	37
19	d	7	1	52
20	d	8	1	125
21	e	8	1	124
22	b	9	5	410
23	a	9	5	410

Question number	Answer	KSA number	Reference	Page number
24	a	9	5	424
25	b	9	5	424
26	d	9	5	424
27	c	9	5	357
28	a	9	3	1368
29	a	9	3	324
30	e	10	1	169
31	d	10	1	173
32	a	11	2	242
33	e	11	2	242
34	b	11	2	241
35	a	11	2	243
36	d	11	2	243
37	b	11	2	243
38	d	11	2	244
39	d	11	1	199
40	c	12	1	213
41	d	12	2	251
42	b	12	2	251
43	e	12	1	213-214
44	a	12	1	214
45	a	12	1	212

CHAPTER 8

Human Behavior and Psychology

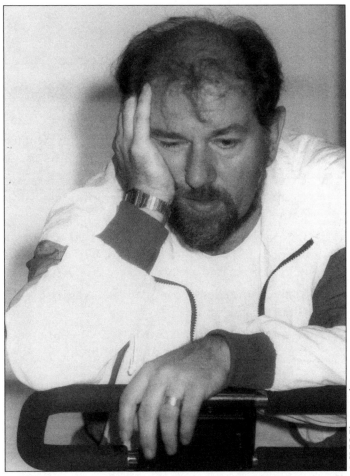

© CLEO Photography

The emphasis of this ACSM KSA category, Human Behavior and Psychology, is effective communication primarily for the purpose of changing health behaviors. It is essential that the Health/Fitness Instructor know how to deal effectively with various personalities when implementing programs designed to improve exercise adherence as well as other targeted health behaviors such as those related to smoking, diet, and stress management. You are likely to receive four questions from this category. We suggest that you begin your study of this KSA category by consulting chapter 8 in the fourth edition of *Guidelines for Exercise Testing and Prescription* (ACSM, 1991). Note that this important chapter was omitted in the most recent edition (ACSM, 1995).

PRACTICE QUESTIONS

Directions: Each question is followed by either four or five possible answers. Select the *best* answer to the question.

 1. What should the exercise professional do first when dealing with a chronic complainer during a group exercise session?

   a. Determine whether or not the client is a true chronic complainer or someone who is simply looking for a sympathetic ear.

   b. Ignore the negative behavior for two weeks since the client may not be a chronic problem and the negative behavior may go away on its own.

   c. Listen to the client's complaints and agree to correct the client's concerns.

   d. Assign a staff member to exercise with the client to keep the chronic complainer under control.

 2. Which of the following strategies is (are) useful for dealing with a client who fails to adhere to your group exercise program protocol?

   a. Determine why the client fails to cooperate.

   b. Use negative reinforcement in an attempt to correct the client's behavior.

    c. Work with the client to set realistic incremental goals.

    d. *a* and *b*

    e. *a* and *c*

B 3. Which of the following is most important when setting exercise goals for the beginning participant?

    a. Set and emphasize long-term goals (six months) in order to motivate the participant to adhere to the exercise program.

    b. Set and emphasize short-term goals of approximately one to two weeks.

    c. Avoid establishing exercise goals until the participant has been in the program for at least two months.

    d. Avoid establishing exercise goals until the participant has been in the program for at least three months.

B 4. What term is used to identify any action implemented during or after the occurrence of a behavior that increases the probability that the behavior will occur again?

    a. goal-setting

    b. reinforcement

    c. shaping

    d. stimulus-control

C 5. What is the term for a health behavior change strategy that recognizes the need to change health behavior gradually?

    a. cognitive behavior

    b. contracting

    c. shaping

    d. self-management

E 6. Which of the following is (are) most important as an indication that an exercise leader is effective?

    a. Participants believe the exercise leader is competent.

    b. Participants believe the exercise leader likes and understands their needs.

c. The exercise leader persistently (month after month) attempts to talk participants into making major lifestyle behavioral changes.

d. *a* and *b*

e. *a, b,* and *c*

 7. What name is given to a relaxation technique characterized by instructions to contract a specific muscle or muscle group followed by a conscious relaxation of the muscle or muscle group, with particular attention to differences in the degree of tension in the muscles?

a. autogenic training

b. Benson's relaxation response

c. cognitive restructuring

d. progressive relaxation

8. Which of the following are indications of relaxed breathing?

a. Chest rises and abdomen moves inward during inhalation.

b. Abdomen rises during inhalation and falls during exhalation.

c. The number of breaths per minute is 8-12.

d. *a* and *c*

e. *b* and *c*

 9. What name is given to a form of relaxation training that is characterized by the use of suggestive subvocal phrases involving states of heaviness, warmth, heat, respiration, and solar plexus and forehead tension?

a. autogenic training

b. cognitive restructuring

c. progressive relaxation

d. quieting-reflex training

_A_ 10. What exercise performance awards are extrinsic in nature?

    a. jogging a total of 100 miles in three months and receiving a free T-shirt

    b. a good feeling of accomplishment for having jogged 100 miles in three months

    c. a good feeling of accomplishment for having lost 4 pounds in one month

    d. a good feeling of accomplishment for increasing HDL-C by 5 mg/dl

    e. *b, c,* and *d*

_C_ 11. Which health behavioral change principle is most effective for encouraging exercise adherence over the long term?

    a. generalization training

    b. self-management

    c. social support

    d. contracting

_B_ 12. Which personal strategy should people implement as soon as possible after a lapse (minimum of three weeks) in exercise adherence?

    a. Instruct the exercise professional to write a new exercise contract.

    b. Recall self-management strategies.

    c. Be realistic and admit that they failed.

    d. Force themselves to exercise at a high intensity to make up for lost time.

_D_ 13. What is the correct order of the stages that describe a health behavioral change model used to help a potential exercise participant initiate, adhere to, and maintain an exercise program?

    a. adoption, maintenance, antecedents

    b. antecedents, adoption, maintenance

    c. adoption, antecedents, maintenance

    d. none of the above

_A_ 14. Which of the following health behavioral change strategies is (are) useful for helping a client maintain exercise adherence?

    a. using a written contract

    b. before the client engages in an exercise program, requiring him/her to develop an exercise relapse prevention program

    c. making the participant feel guilty if he/she contemplates stopping the exercise program

    d. *a* and *b*

    e. *b* and *c*

_D_ 15. To effectively change behavior, what should the exercise leader convince the exercise participant to do?

    a. Establish realistic short-term and long-term goals.

    b. Sign a contract.

    c. Recognize the importance of never missing an exercise session during the first six weeks of the exercise program.

    d. *a* and *b*

    e. *a* and *c*

_D_ 16. What personality trait(s) may cause exercise participants to overexert themselves?

    a. aggression

    b. assertiveness

    c. denial

    d. *a* and *b*

    e. *a, b, c,* and *d*

_A_ 17. What personality type is characterized by hostility, competitive behavior, and hard-driving attitude?

    a. type A

    b. type B

    c. type C

    d. type D

D 18. What symptom(s) of depression often make(s) it difficult to maintain exercise adherence?

a. crying easily

b. suicidal feelings

c. slight swelling above the ear in the region of the temporal bone

d. *a* and *b*

e. *b* and *c*

E 19. What symptom(s) of anxiety often make(s) it difficult to maintain exercise adherence?

a. dyspnea

b. chest pain

c. muscle tension

d. *a* and *b*

e. *b* and *c*

C 20. What should the exercise leader do when an exercise participant offers an excuse for his/her inactivity?

a. Accept the excuses as fact.

b. Ask the participant whether or not he/she is telling the truth.

c. Continue to communicate with the participant until the real reasons are uncovered.

d. Tell the participant that the excuse is questionable and that he/she may be asked to leave the exercise program.

A 21. When should resting HR and BP readings be taken to help ensure that a true resting measurement is obtained?

a. on a day in which no exercise test is planned

b. 1 minute prior to the exercise test while the client sits on the cycle ergometer

c. 5 minutes prior to the exercise test while the client sits on the cycle ergometer

d. 10 minutes prior to the exercise test while the client sits on the cycle ergometer

_C_   22. Which of the following best describes preexercise anticipatory responses?

    a. increased HR, vasodilatation in the gut region, increased arterial BP, and increased myocardial contractility

    b. increased HR, vasoconstriction in the gut region, decreased arterial BP, and increased myocardial contractility

    c. increased HR, vasoconstriction in the gut region, increased arterial BP, and increased myocardial contractility

    d. decreased HR, vasoconstriction in the gut region, decreased arterial BP, and decreased myocardial contractility

_D_   23. Which of the following is an *ineffective* method of long-term body composition management?

    a. modifying behavior

    b. changing the client's "thoughts" regarding the role and purpose of food

    c. exercising on a consistent basis

    d. maintaining a very low calorie diet

REFERENCES FOR FURTHER STUDY

1. ACSM. (1991). *Guidelines for exercise testing and prescription* (4th ed.). Malvern, PA: Lea & Febiger.

2. ACSM. (1993). *ACSM's resource manual for guidelines for exercise testing and prescription* (2nd ed.). Malvern, PA: Lea & Febiger.

3. Howley, E.T., & Franks, B.D. (1997). *Health fitness instructor's handbook* (3rd ed.). Champaign, IL: Human Kinetics.

4. McArdle, W.D., Katch, F.I., & Katch, V.L. (1991). *Exercise physiology: Energy, nutrition, and human performance* (3rd ed.). Philadelphia, PA: Lea & Febiger.

ANSWERS

Question number	Answer	KSA number	Reference	Page number
1	a	1	2	440
2	e	1	2	441
3	b	2	1	189
4	b	2	1	189
5	c	2	1	189
X 6	d	3	2	434
7	d	4	2	496
X 8	e	4	2	498
9	a	4	2	497
10	a	5	2	448
X 11	b	6	1	191
12	b	6	1	192
X 13	b	6	2	430
X 14	d	6	2	433
15	d	7	3	397
X 16	e	8	3	378
17	a	8	3	377
18	d	8	2	438
X 19	d	8	2	438
20	c	8	3	199
21	a	9	4	317
22	c	9	4	322
23	d	11	2	462

Health Appraisal and Fitness Testing

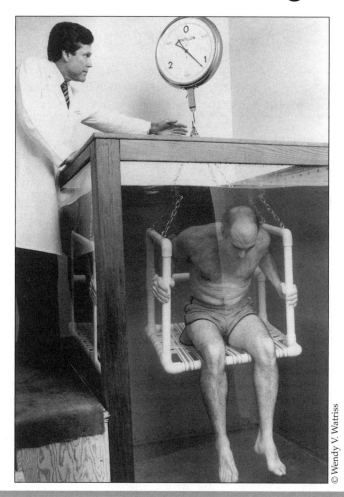

While the ACSM KSA category Health Appraisal and Fitness Testing consists of only 24 objectives, you will likely encounter as many as 12 questions from this category. To obtain a passing score, it is mandatory that you put to memory most of the information we presented in table 1.2 (see chapter 1, p. 10). Pay particular attention to the information regarding informed consent, absolute and relative indications for terminating an exercise test, recommendations for medical exam and exercise testing before participation, and recommendations for physician's supervision of an exercise test, as well as information related to individual test procedures. In chapter 15 we provide additional practice questions directly relating to this KSA category, written in the form of case studies.

PRACTICE QUESTIONS

Directions: Each question is followed by either four or five possible answers. Select the *best* answer to the question.

1. Mr. Smith is a 39-year-old smoker who maintains an active lifestyle. Information obtained from a medical history and physical examination revealed the following: BP 141/91; total serum cholesterol 180; high-density lipoprotein 61; father died of a heart attack at 64 years of age. What is Mr. Smith's initial risk stratification?
   a. apparently healthy
   b. increased risk
   c. known disease
   d. unknown

2. What should an informed consent include?
   a. an explanation of the tests to be administered, possible risks and discomforts, possible medications the participant can take and cannot take prior to exercise testing, freedom of consent, signatures of both the participant and a witness
   b. an explanation of the test to be administered, possible risks and discomforts, benefits to be expected, freedom of consent, signature of the participant

    c. an explanation of the tests to be administered, possible risks and discomforts, benefits to be expected, freedom of consent, signatures of both the participant and a witness

    d. an explanation of the tests to be administered, possible risks and discomforts, the participant's responsibilities, benefits to be expected, inquiries, freedom of consent, signatures of both the participant and a witness

    e. None of the above contain all the important elements needed in an informed consent.

3. Which statement is true regarding informed consent?

    a. It should be obtained before an exercise test and before participation in an exercise program.

    b. It should be obtained before an exercise test but is not needed prior to exercise program participation.

    c. It should be sent to the potential exercise participant, and the signed form should be mailed to the exercise program director one week prior to program participation.

    d. It should include an explanation of medications the participant should take to reduce muscle soreness.

4. What are the correct directions for administering the Cooper 12-minute test of aerobic capacity?

    a. Mark the track by placing marker cones every 40-55 yards.

    b. Instruct the participants to run, not walk, for the entire 12 minutes.

    c. Instruct the participants to walk, not run, for the entire 12 minutes.

    d. *a* and *b*

    e. *a* and *c*

5. Which of the following represents a rank order of the most accurate technique to the least accurate technique for determining body composition?

    a. hydrostatic, skinfold, anthropometric, bioelectrical impedance, infrared interactance

   b. hydrostatic, anthropometric, skinfold, infrared inter-
     actance, bioelectrical impedance

   c. hydrostatic, skinfold, anthropometric, infrared inter-
     actance, bioelectrical impedance

   d. infrared interactance, skinfold, bioelectrical impedance,
     anthropometric, hydrostatic

   e. bioelectrical impedance, hydrostatic, anthropometric,
     infrared interactance

6. Of the following tests, which one relies upon HR recovery as an indicator of cardiorespiratory fitness?

   a. YMCA submaximal cycle ergometry protocol

   b. YMCA three-minute step test

   c. Harvard step test

   d. Rockport 1-mile fitness walk

7. Barring complications, a submaximal treadmill exercise test is often terminated when the client obtains a predetermined HR endpoint of what percentage of predicted maximal HRR?

   a. 55

   b. 65

   c. 75

   d. 85

   e. 95

8. Of the five Korotkoff sounds (phases), which is considered to represent SBP in adults?

   a. 1

   b. 2

   c. 3

   d. 4

   e. 5

9. As an exercise professional, what should you direct an apparently healthy 35-year-old male, interested in

beginning a low- to moderate-intensity exercise program, to do first?

a. Receive a physician's clearance.

b. Contact a cardiologist to take a GXT.

c. Take the Physical Activity Readiness Questionnaire.

d. Take the Cooper 12-minute run test.

10. Which of the following individuals should receive medical clearance before participating in a vigorous exercise program?

a. a 28-year-old male with one CAD risk factor (no signs or symptoms)

b. a 28-year-old female with one CAD risk factor (no signs or symptoms)

c. a 46-year-old male (no signs or symptoms)

d. a 46-year-old female (no signs or symptoms)

e. None of the above individuals needs prior medical clearance.

11. Of the following, which is not an absolute contraindication to exercise testing?

a. uncontrolled ventricular arrhythmia

b. uncontrolled metabolic disease

c. uncontrolled atrial arrhythmia

d. unstable angina

12. An examination of Ms. Johnson's medical file reveals the following significant facts: complicated pregnancy, unstable angina, and uncontrolled diabetes. Which of these facts, if any, represent absolute contraindications to exercise testing?

a. complicated pregnancy

b. unstable angina

c. unstable angina and uncontrolled diabetes

d. None of the above is an absolute contraindication to exercise testing.

13. What laboratory tests should be obtained before an exercise test involving an individual classified as apparently healthy?

    a. chest x-ray

    b. 12-lead resting ECG

    c. pulmonary function test

    d. total serum cholesterol

    e. *b* and *d*

 14. What is true regarding the limitations of an informed consent form?

    a. A signed informed consent offers no legal protection and therefore should not be incorporated in an exercise program.

    b. All informed consent forms should be reviewed by local legal counsel before implementation.

    c. After signing an informed consent form it is still possible for the professional to be sued.

    d. There are no limitations; once participants have signed the informed consent form they have forfeited their right to sue.

    e. *b* and *c*

 15. For how many hours preceding physical fitness testing should the participant be instructed to avoid food, tobacco, alcohol, and caffeine?

    a. two

    b. three

    c. five

    d. eight

16. What is considered the "gold standard" for determining body composition?

    a. bioelectrical impedance analysis

    b. hydrostatic weighing

    c. infrared interactance

    d. skinfold measurements

_B_ 17. Which of the following best describes the appropriate abdominal skinfold site?

   a. horizonal fold taken 2 centimeters to the left of the umbilicus

   b. vertical fold taken 2 centimeters to the right of the umbilicus

   c. horizonal fold taken 4 centimeters to the left of the umbilicus

   d. vertical fold taken 4 centimeters to the right of the umbilicus

_D_ 18. Which of the following best describes the appropriate medial calf skinfold site?

   a. horizontal fold taken 2 centimeters from the midline of the medial border

   b. vertical fold taken 2 centimeters from the midline of the medial border

   c. horizontal fold taken on the midline of the medial border at a level with the calf's greatest circumference

   d. vertical fold taken on the midline of the medial border at a level with the calf's greatest circumference

_C_ 19. Which of the following best describes the appropriate procedure for obtaining a skinfold measurement?

   a. Measure right side, place caliper 3 centimeters from thumb and finger, and wait three to four seconds before reading caliper.

   b. Measure left side, place caliper 2 centimeters from thumb and finger, and wait one to two seconds before reading caliper.

   c. Measure right side, place caliper 1 centimeter from thumb and finger, and wait one to two seconds before reading caliper.

   d. Measure left side, place caliper 1 centimeter from thumb and finger, and wait one to two seconds before reading caliper.

20. What is a limitation of using bioelectrical impedance analysis?

    a. It overestimates percent body fat in very lean individuals.

    b. It underestimates percent body fat in men.

    c. It underestimates percent body fat in very tall individuals (over 6 feet 4 inches).

    d. It underestimates percent body fat in very short individuals (under 5 feet).

21. Which of the following is required by the YMCA cycle ergometry protocol?

    a. one steady state HR measurement between 90 and 110 beats per minute

    b. one steady state HR measurement between 110 and 150 beats per minute

    c. two steady state HR measurements between 90 and 110 beats per minute

    d. two steady state HR measurements between 110 and 150 beats per minute

22. What should be considered in the selection of an exercise test protocol for an older adult?

    a. allowing a warm-up of more than three minutes

    b. starting the test at a low intensity level of between 2 and 3 METs

    c. increasing the expected exercise time to 18-20 minutes because of the lower starting intensity

    d. *a* and *b*

    e. *b* and *c*

23. Barring an abnormal exercise recovery response, all observations (HR, BP, RPE, signs and symptoms) should continue for at least how many minutes following a submaximal cycle ergometer exercise test?

    a. two

    b. four

c. six

d. eight

24. At what times during a submaximal cycle ergometer exercise test utilizing three-minute stages should BP be monitored?

a. first portion of each minute

b. last portion of each minute

c. first portion of each stage

d. later portion of each stage

25. What minimal baseline measures should be obtained prior to the start of an exercise test for an apparently healthy individual?

a. resting HR

b. resting BP

c. resting ECG

d. *a* and *b*

e. *b* and *c*

26. When BP is being measured, the cuff should be deflated at what rate of mm Hg per second?

a. 1

b. 2-3

c. 5-6

d. 7-8

27. When BP is being measured, the cuff should be quickly inflated how many mm Hg above the SBP?

a. 10-20

b. 20-30

c. 30-40

d. 40-50

e. 50-60

_C_ 28. Which of the following correctly describes the procedure for calibrating a Monark cycle ergometer?

   a. Place the cycle on a level surface, attach a 0.5-kilogram weight to the flywheel's belt and spring, pedal at a rate of 50 rev/min, and note whether or not the pendulum moves to the 0.5-kilogram mark.

   b. Place the cycle on a 0.5 percent incline, attach a 0.5-kilogram weight to the flywheel's spring, pedal at a rate of 50 rev/min, and note whether or not the pendulum moves to the 0.5-kilogram mark.

   c. Place the cycle on a level surface, disconnect the flywheel belt, attach a 0.5-kilogram weight to the flywheel's spring, and note whether or not the pendulum moves to the 0.5-kilogram mark.

   d. Place the cycle on a level surface, disconnect the flywheel belt, attach a 0.5-kilogram weight to the flywheel's spring, pedal at a rate of 50 rev/min, and note whether or not the pendulum moves to the 0.5-kilogram mark.

_D_ 29. Which of the following BP responses would represent a general indication to discontinue a GXT in an apparently
_A_   healthy adult?

   a. SBP drops 15 mm Hg with an increase in exercise intensity.

   b. SBP rises to 240 mm Hg.

   c. DBP fails to increase with an increase in exercise intensity.

   d. *a* and *c*

_B_ 30. General indication for discontinuing a GXT in apparently healthy adults would include all but which one of the following?

   a. Subject asks to stop test.

   b. Subject's HR increases to 170 beats per minute.

   c. Subject shows manifestations of severe fatigue.

   d. Subject's HR fails to increase with an increase in exercise intensity.

REFERENCES FOR FURTHER STUDY

1. ACSM. (1993). *ACSM's resource manual for guidelines for exercise testing and prescription* (2nd ed.). Malvern, PA: Lea & Febiger.

2. ACSM. (1995). *ACSM's guidelines for exercise testing and prescription* (5th ed.). Baltimore: Williams & Wilkins.

3. American Heart Association. (1987). *Recommendations for human blood pressure determination by sphygmomanometer.* Dallas: American Heart Association.

4. Maud, P.J., & Foster, C. (Eds.). (1995). *Physiological assessment of human fitness.* Champaign, IL: Human Kinetics.

5. Safrit, M.J., & Wood, T.M. (1995). *Introduction to measurement in physical education and exercise science.* (3rd ed.). St. Louis: Mosby.

ANSWERS

Question number	Answer	KSA number	Reference	Page number
1	a	1	2	18
2	d	2	2	43
3	a	2	2	41
4	a	3	4	42
5	a	5	2	53-63
6	c	5	5	496
7	d	6	2	73
8	a	8	3	4
9	c	9	2	13
10	c	11	2	25
11	b	12	2	42
12	b	12	2	42
13	d	13	2	32
14	e	14	1	536

Question number	Answer	KSA number	Reference	Page number
15	b	15	2	51
16	b	17	2	53
17	b	17	2	56
18	d	17	2	56
19	c	17	2	56
20	a	17	2	62
21	d	18	2	68
22	d	19	2	230
23	b	20	2	70
24	d	20	2	70
25	d	20	2	75
26	b	21	1	576
27	b	21	1	576
28	c	23	1	549
29	a	24	2	78
30	b	24	2	78

CHAPTER 10

Emergency Procedures and Safety

© W. Lynn Seldon

This chapter contains 34 practice questions to help you study for the 13 objectives listed under the ACSM certification KSAs in the category titled Emergency Procedures and Safety. Pay close attention to the "demonstrate" objectives, as you will likely be tested on this information in your practical exam. On the basis of previous ACSM Health/Fitness Instructor certification examinations, you are likely to receive approximately eight questions from this category.

Before taking the certification exam, you must provide documentation showing that you have successfully completed a CPR course. We also recommend taking a standard first aid course. Your CPR and first aid training, review of these materials, and correctly answering the questions contained within this chapter will adequately prepare you to take this portion of the certification examination.

PRACTICE QUESTIONS

Directions: Each question is followed by either four or five possible answers. Select the *best* answer to the question.

1. What activities are required in order for one to receive a certificate in basic life support and CPR?
   a. performing specific skills completely and demonstrating the ability to make appropriate decisions for care
   b. passing a final written exam
   c. participating in 80 hours of practicum work
   d. *a* and *b*
   e. *a, b,* and *c*

2. What is the correct order of events to find the correct hand position in CPR for the adult?
   a. Use the heel of your hand to apply pressure on the sternum; find the lower edge of the victim's rib cage; place the heel of one hand on the sternum next to your index finger and place your other hand on top of it; slide your middle and index fingers up to the edge of the rib cage to the notch where the ribs meet the sternum; place your middle and index fingers on the notch where the ribs meet the sternum.

b. Find the lower edge of the victim's rib cage; place the heel of one hand on the sternum next to your index finger and place your other hand on top of it; use the heel of your hand to apply pressure on the sternum; slide your middle and index fingers up the edge of the rib cage to the notch where the ribs meet the sternum; place your middle and index fingers on the notch where the ribs meet the sternum.

c. Find the lower edge of the victim's rib cage; slide your middle and index fingers up the edge of the rib cage to the notch where the ribs meet the sternum; place the heel of one hand on the sternum next to your index finger and place your other hand on top of it; place your middle and index fingers on the notch where the ribs meet the sternum; use the heel of your hand to apply pressure on the sternum.

d. Find the lower edge of the victim's rib cage; slide your middle and index fingers up the edge of the rib cage to the notch where the ribs meet the sternum; place your middle and index fingers on the notch where the ribs meet the sternum; place the heel of one hand on the sternum next to your index finger and place your other hand on top of it; use the heel of your hand to apply pressure on the sternum.

3. All personnel must know what about the facility's emergency plan?

   a. how to activate it

   b. the location of the telephone and emergency number

   c. the location of all emergency equipment

   d. *a* and *b*

   e. *a, b,* and *c*

4. At a facility such as a YMCA, a pool, or a local community park without emergency equipment, what is the responsibility of the first rescuer in a potentially life-threatening situation?

   a. to establish responsiveness of the victim

   b. to check for bleeding from the victim

c. to call the EMS

d. *a* and *b*

e. *a*, *b*, and *c*

5. At a gym or exercise facility with basic emergency equipment (defibrillator, drugs, etc.), what is the responsibility of the second rescuer on the scene in a potentially life-threatening situation?

a. to call the EMS

b. to wait to direct the emergency team

c. to bring all emergency equipment to the scene of the accident

d. *a* and *b*

e. *a*, *b*, and *c*

6. What is the first-aid procedure for bleeding?

a. covering the wound with a clean dressing and pressing firmly against the wound with the hand

b. elevating the wound (preferably above the level of the heart)

c. applying a tourniquet when the bleeding is serious

d. *a* and *b*

e. *a*, *b*, and *c*

7. What should be done if a person experiences dizziness or syncope?

a. Place the victim on his/her side.

b. Give the victim some form of sugar, preferably in liquid form.

c. Position the victim on his/her back and elevate the legs 8 to 10 inches (only if there is no suspected head or back injury).

d. Restrain the individual and place a bit block between the teeth.

8. What is the first aid for a diabetic emergency?

   a. giving the individual oral insulin

   b. giving the individual oral glucose (or other form of sugar)

   c. giving the victim water and transporting him/her to the hospital

   d. placing the victim on his/her side in case there is vomiting

X 9. First aid for heat exhaustion includes all but which of the following?

   C   a. removing the victim from the sun to a ventilated and cooler area

   b. placing the victim in shock position

   c. transporting the victim to the hospital immediately

   d. forcing fluids to lower the body temperature

E 10. Of the following, which demonstrate(s) that the risks associated with physical activity are low?

   a. Studies of exercise in apparently healthy adults report an incidence of a sudden cardiac event as 1 per 187,500 hours of exercise per person.

   b. The death rate for male joggers is 1 per 396,000 hours of jogging.

   c. The incidence of cardiac arrest among male joggers is 1 per 18,000 joggers.

   d. *a* and *b*

   e. *a, b,* and *c*

D 11. What is the risk of death in cardiac rehabilitation programs?

   a. approximately 1 death per 120,000 patient hours

   b. approximately one event every 112,000 hours

   c. one event per year in individuals exercising fewer than three times per week

   d. *a* and *b*

   e. *a, b,* and *c*

___ 12. Of the following signs/symptoms observed during an exercise session, all but which one would warrant termination of the session?

    a. angina pectoris

    b. syncope

    c. pain in the jaw or neck

    d. beads of sweat forming on the forehead

    e. excessive air hunger

___ 13. Which of the following is (are) suggested as a guideline(s) to terminate an exercise session?

    a. fatigue

    b. failure of the monitoring equipment

    c. > 20 mm Hg drop in SBP

    d. *a* and *b*

    e. *a*, *b*, and *c*

___ 14. The design and layout of a weight room should adhere to which of the following guidelines to assure participant safety?

    a. Each piece of exercise equipment should have 20-40 square feet of area.

    b. There should be 20-25 square feet of space for each person using the floor area.

    c. The floor should be covered with an antistatic carpet pretreated for bacterial and fungal agents.

    d. *a* and *b*

    e. *a*, *b*, and *c*

___ 15. What is required to maintain the safety of the participant in a weight room?

    a. an ongoing maintenance program to monitor all equipment

    b. supervision of the area by individuals who have expertise at the Exercise Leader, Health/Fitness Instructor, or Director level

c. a safe entry to the area that is at least 3 feet wide and is in accordance with local, state, and federal laws

d. *a* and *b*

e. *a, b,* and *c*

16. A 65-year-old male is working out in the fitness facility on a bicycle ergometer. He begins to feel light-headed and nauseous. His speech is slurred. He collapses. You are on the exercise floor and observe this situation. What should you do?

a. Make sure the victim is lying down, and check the airway and circulation.

b. Call the EMS.

c. Call the EMS and go to the entrance and wait for the ambulance.

d. Give CPR immediately.

17. You are helping out with an exercise test on a 50-year-old female with moderate valvular heart disease. During the test, she complains of uncomfortable chest pain (3.0 on the angina scale). It is the decision of the physician to stop the test. What should you do?

a. Assist the physician and the exercise physiologist/clinical exercise specialist.

b. Bring all the emergency equipment to the area.

c. Call the EMS.

d. *a* and *b*

e. *a, b,* and *c*

18. You are supervising the running track where participants are walking and jogging. One of the walkers wanders from his designated walking lane into the path of a jogger absorbed in conversation. The walker is accidentally pushed to the floor of the track. What should you do?

a. Assess the injured individual(s).

b. Treat the injured individual(s) in the facility or send for the outside community resource (paramedic, fire department, etc.).

c. Call EMS immediately and send someone to the entrance to wait.

d. *a* and *b*

e. *a*, *b*, and *c*

19. Which of the following reduce(s) the possibility of injury in a health/fitness facility and help(s) create a safe environment in which to work?

a. advance planning of exercise sessions to follow the FIT principle

b. keeping equipment well maintained and making sure that exercise areas are clean and well lit when in use

c. providing appropriate exercise-based counseling to participants upon completion of preliminary screening and testing

d. *a* and *b*

e. *a*, *b*, and *c*

20. What is required to maintain a safe environment in an exercise/fitness facility?

a. easy access to emergency exits and monitoring equipment (if used at the facility)

b. a comfortable environment in which to work or exercise (heat, light, humidity)

c. floors with shock-absorbing material on areas used for impact activities and running

d. a physician on call

21. Which of the following is (are) required in a well-written informed consent?

a. a clear description of the program and procedures

b. a clear description of the potential benefits and risks of the program

c. a statement of individual anonymity

d. *a* and *b*

e. *a*, *b*, and *c*

C 22. With regard to informed consent and its legal considerations, which of the following could result in some form of
a legal claim?

    a. failure of the facility to obtain a release form from the
physician

    b. failure of the facility to give the participant a notarized
copy of the signed informed consent form

    c. failure of the facility to explain the procedures and risks
associated with exercise or any evaluation test

    d. failure of the facility to have two witnesses sign the
informed consent document

X *A*
  B 23. For the exercise professional, being accused of "failure to
respond adequately to an untoward event with appropriate
emergency care" is a claim that could most likely result in
which one of the following?

    a. participant withdrawal from the fitness program

    b. litigation procedures against the Health/Fitness Instruc-
tor and/or the facility

    c. loss of employment for the Health/Fitness Instructor

    d. an increase in liability insurance for the Health/Fitness
Instructor

X *E*
  B 24. In a fitness facility, it is the employer's responsibility to have
documented guidelines on emergency procedures and to
properly communicate these to all employees. What is the
responsibility of the Health/Fitness Instructor?

    a. to evaluate and render a diagnosis of a medical con-
dition or accident once appropriate training has been
obtained

    b. to make sure that emergency training is obtained and
updated to prevent careless performance in an emergency situation

    c. to assign someone to carry out emergency care accord-
ing to the instructions in the facility legal document

    d. *a* and *b*

    e. *a*, *b*, and *c*

E 25. For the instructor to be protected from liability in all emergency-response situations, what must the employer (facility) do?

    a. Communicate to the instructor the emergency medical procedures.

    b. Provide for appropriate training and updates.

    c. Put the emergency plan into action with periodic drills (at least two times per year).

    d. *a* and *b*

    e. *a, b,* and *c*

A 26. Which of the following matches the musculoskeletal injury to its description?

    a. contusion–slight bleeding into tissues while the skin remains unbroken

    b. sprain–tearing of a muscle or tendon

    c. strain–tearing of ligamentous tissue

    d. fracture–displacement of a particular bone from its normal position

D 27. Cardiovascular/pulmonary complications can include which of the following?

    a. tachycardia–myocardial contraction rate of more than 100 beats per minute; bradycardia–myocardial contraction rate of less than 60 beats per minute

    b. hypotension–a condition in which BP is inadequate for normal perfusion and oxygenation of the tissues; hypertension–a major risk factor for CAD, stroke, congestive heart failure, and chronic renal failure

    c. hypoventilation–a pulmonary ventilation rate that is metabolically necessary for exchange of pulmonary gases; tachypnea–an abnormally rapid rate of breathing as seen in fever

    d. *a* and *b*

    e. *a, b,* and *c*

B 28. Which of the following correctly match(es) the following metabolic abnormalities to the corresponding descriptions?

    a. hyperthermia–body temperature below normal; hypothermia–low body temperature due to exposure to cold temperature

    b. fainting–a loss of consciousness; syncope–a brief lapse in consciousness caused by a decrease in O_2 to the brain

    c. hyperglycemia–a less-than-normal amount of glucose in the blood caused by administration of too much insulin; hypoglycemia–a greater-than-normal amount of glucose in the blood

    d. *a* and *b*

    e. *a, b,* and *c*

D 29. What immediate care is appropriate for most open wounds?

    a. application of direct pressure over the site to stop bleeding

    b. application of a sterile dressing to protect the wound from contamination

    c. maintenance of an open airway

    d. *a* and *b*

    e. *a, b,* and *c*

 30. For injuries to the muscle and joints, appropriate first-aid care would include which of the following?

    a. stopping activity and keeping the victim from applying any weight-bearing to the affected limb

    b. the use of a blanket-type splint for the foot and elevation of the limb

    c. the application of ice and compression to the injury

    d. *a* and *b*

    e. *a, b,* and *c*

31. A 12-year-old female started coughing and wheezing, unable to catch her breath while running on an indoor track. What immediate first aid is appropriate?

    a. maintenance of an open airway

    b. administering or helping the girl administer her oral bronchodilator medication

    c. rushing her to the hospital

    d. *a* and *b*

    e. *a, b,* and *c*

 32. You are supervising the weight room when you hear a young male crying out in pain. An Olympic weight has been dropped on his leg; the bone is protruding and there is bleeding. Precaution for management of this emergency involving blood includes what action(s)?

    a. putting on latex gloves before touching any surface of the body

    b. washing your hands with soap and water immediately after the incident

    c. using a bleach solution to wash all areas of the facility exposed to the accident

    d. *a* and *b*

    e. *a, b,* and *c*

33. A preventive maintenance/repair program for weight-training equipment would involve which of the following procedures?

    a. daily–clean upholstery with a mild soap-and-water solution

    b. weekly–use a vinyl upholstery protectant on all equipment

    c. monthly–inspect cables, nuts, and bolts of all weight machines utilizing such devices

    d. *a* and *b*

    e. *a, b,* and *c*

34. A cardiovascular equipment preventative maintenance/ repair schedule would include which of the following daily procedures?

a. cleaning monorail of the rower machines; washing the seat of the rower with a mild soap-and-water solution

b. cleaning the seat and frame of the bicycle ergometer with a mild soap-and-water solution

c. inspecting the housing, belts, and electronic components on each of the stair climbers

d. *a* and *b*

e. *a*, *b*, and *c*

REFERENCES FOR FURTHER STUDY

1. ACSM. (1991). *Guidelines for exercise testing and prescription* (4th ed.). Malvern, PA: Lea & Febiger.

2. ACSM. (1993). *ACSM's resource manual for guidelines for exercise testing and prescription* (2nd ed.). Malvern, PA: Lea & Febiger.

3. ACSM. (1995). *ACSM's guidelines for exercise testing and prescription* (5th ed.). Baltimore: Williams & Wilkins.

4. American Red Cross. (1993). *CPR for the professional rescuer.* St. Louis: Mosby Lifeline.

5. American Red Cross. (1993). *Responding to emergencies.* St. Louis: Mosby Lifeline.

6. American Red Cross. (1993). *Standard first aid.* St. Louis: Mosby Lifeline.

7. Anderson, K.N. (Ed). (1994). *Mosby's medical, nursing, and allied health dictionary* (4th ed.). St. Louis: Mosby.

8. Howley, E.T., & Franks, B.D. (1997). *Health fitness instructor's handbook* (3rd ed.). Champaign, IL: Human Kinetics.

9. Sol, N., & Foster, C. (Eds.). (1992). *Hospital health promotion.* Champaign, IL: Human Kinetics.

ANSWERS

Question number	Answer	KSA number	Reference	Page number
1	d	1	4	xii
			3	253
2	d	1	5	118
3	e	2	2	367
			3	255
4	d	2	2	375
5	c	2	2	375
6	d	3	8	412
			6	144
7	c	3	6	194
			5	282
8	b	3	8	421
			5	283
9	c	3	8	414
			5	337
10	e	4	3	8
11	d	4	2	362
12	d	5	2	362
13	e	5	2	367
			1	127
14	e	6	9	72
15	e	6	9	71
16	a	7	2	376
			5	286

Question number	Answer	KSA number	Reference	Page number
17	d	7	2	375
18	d	7	9	30
19	e	8	8	407
20	b	8	2	368
21	d	9	3	41
			2	230, 366, 532
			8	463
22	c	9	3	41
			2	230, 366, 532
23	b	10	2	536
24	b	10	9	23
25	e	10	9	29
26	a	11	5	209
			8	410
27	d	11	2	67, 187, 276
			7	778, 779, 1524
			8	421, 441
28	b	11	8	361, 414, 418, 421
			5	282, 284, 333, 373
29	d	12	2	373
			5	170
			8	412
30	e	12	2	373
			5	209
			8	422
31	d	12	2	193, 373

Question number	Answer	KSA number	Reference	Page number
			5	75
			8	364
32	e	13	9	31
33	e	13	9	140
34	d	13	9	142

CHAPTER 11

Exercise Programming

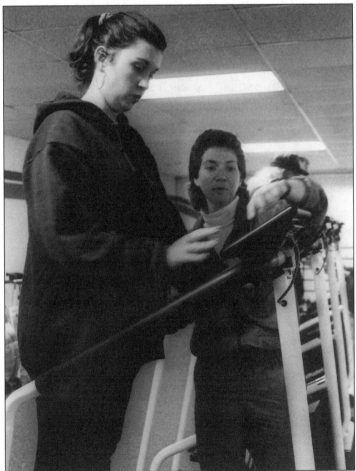

© CLEO Photography

Of the 10 ACSM KSA categories, Exercise Programming is the most comprehensive. This KSA category consists of 46 objectives, many of which contain multiple components. When studying, be sure you understand each component of the objective before moving on to the next objective. Based on previous ACSM Health/Fitness Instructor certification examinations, you are likely to receive approximately 11 questions from this category.

PRACTICE QUESTIONS

> Directions: Each question is followed by either four or five possible answers. Select the *best* answer to the question.

 1. What mode of prolonged exercise is most likely to produce significant improvement in maximal aerobic capacity?

   a. rhythmic small-muscle activity

   b. rhythmic large-muscle activity

   c. nonrhythmic small-muscle activity

   d. nonrhythmic large-muscle activity

 2. What intensity of exercise is needed to develop CRF in an apparently healthy individual?

   a. 40-60 percent of maximum HR

   b. 60-90 percent of maximum HR

   c. 50-85 percent of HRR

   d. *a* and *c*

   e. *b* and *c*

 3. What does the ACSM recommend regarding the duration of exercise for the development of CRF?

   a. high-intensity (>90 percent) exercise for 5-10 minutes

   b. multiple 10-minute exercise sessions for the severely deconditioned

   c. continuous aerobic activity for 20-60 minutes

   d. *a* and *b*

   e. *b* and *c*

_D_ 4. What does the ACSM recommend regarding the frequency of cardiorespiratory exercise?

    a. one to two sessions per week for individuals who possess a 3-5 MET capacity

    b. one to two sessions per day for individuals who possess a 3-5 MET capacity

    c. three to five sessions per day for individuals who possess a > 5 MET capacity

    d. three to five sessions per week for individuals who possess a > 5 MET capacity

_C_ 5. Which statement best describes the movement known as "exercise lite"?

    a. Every adult should accumulate 15 minutes or more of moderate-intensity physical activity over the course of most days.

    b. Every adult should accumulate 15 minutes or more of high-intensity physical activity over the course of most days.

    c. Every adult should accumulate 30 minutes or more of moderate-intensity physical activity over the course of most days.

    d. Every adult should accumulate 30 minutes or more of high-intensity physical activity over the course of most days.

 X _A_ 6. What is required to maintain, as opposed to improve, a given level of muscular strength?

    a. increasing training volume and decreasing training intensity

    b. increasing training volume and increasing training intensity

    c. decreasing training volume and decreasing training intensity

    d. decreasing training volume and increasing training intensity

X A 7. How long does the "improvement stage" of a CRF exercise
B   training program typically last?

   a. four to six weeks
   b. four to five months
   c. one year
   d. two years

X A 8. During the improvement stage of a CRF exercise training
       program, how often is the duration of exercise increased
B   until the performer is capable of exercising continuously for
       20-30 minutes?

   a. every week
   b. every two to three weeks
   c. every five weeks
   d. by one minute for each subsequent workout session

C 9. What procedure is most appropriate during the mainte-
      nance stage of a CRF exercise training program?

   a. Exercise intensity is generally increased by 1 percent per
      week.
   b. Exercise duration is generally increased by one minute
      per exercise session.
   c. A new exercise program similar in energy cost to the
      original conditioning program should be developed
      and implemented.
   d. The participant should attempt to improve CRF by no
      more than an additional 12 percent.

A 10. Placing a muscle or muscle group under a stress greater
       than it is accustomed to handling is an example of what
       principle?

   a. overload
   b. specificity
   c. isotonic resistance
   d. isokinetic resistance

C or A 11. Select the term(s) that best represent(s) the following:
           using high-intensity, low-volume resistance training for the

development of muscular strength, as well as using low-intensity, high-volume resistance training for the development of muscular endurance.

a. the overload principle

b. progressive resistance

c. the principle of specificity

d. *a* and *b*

A 12. Which of the following exercises would have the greatest carry-over effect (specificity) for a throwing event activity?

a. lat pull-over

b. push-up

c. bench press

d. power clean

A 13. What should be incorporated with warm-up exercises performed prior to sport participation?

a. a general warm-up followed by a sport-specific warm-up

b. a sport-specific warm-up followed by a general warm-up

c. only a general warm-up

d. only a sport-specific warm-up

C 14. Which of the following is *not* a value of a cooldown period following an exercise session?

a. It aids in the removal of by-products of strenuous exercise.

b. It aids in the prevention of venous pooling in the legs.

c. It reduces the risk of injury.

d. It allows the circulatory system to gradually return to a resting level.

D 15. How does a structured warm-up prior to an exercise session prepare the body for additional intense activity?

a. It increases muscle blood flow and muscle temperature.

b. It increases connective tissue elasticity.

c. It increases muscle viscosity.

d. *a* and *b*

e. *b* and *c*

16. What is the proper exercise sequence among the following activities?

   a. slow jog, static stretching, 2-mile run, 1/4-mile walk, static stretching

   b. slow jog, 2-mile run, 1/4-mile walk

   c. 2-mile run, 1/4-mile walk, static stretching

   d. slow jog, dynamic stretching, 2-mile run, 1/4-mile walk, dynamic stretching

17. Which term best describes a type of muscular contraction that acts as a braking force and involves muscle elongation during tension development?

   a. concentric

   b. isometric

   c. eccentric

   d. isotonic

18. Which of the following is (are) *incorrect* regarding the nature of an eccentric muscle contraction?

   a. muscle elongation during force production

   b. maximum effort not great enough to overcome an external force applied in an opposing direction

   c. a braking force to control speed of movement

   d. less muscle soreness compared to that with a concentric contraction

   e. *b* and *d*

19. What term best describes a type of muscle contraction in which the muscle shortens, causing movement at a joint?

   a. concentric

   b. eccentric

   c. isometric

   d. plyometric

20. What term best describes a type of muscle contraction in which there is no joint movement and no change in the length of the agonist muscle?

a. concentric

b. eccentric

c. isometric

d. isotonic

 21. Which term best describes a type of muscle contraction in which the speed of muscle contraction is precisely controlled?

a. isokinetic

b. isometric

c. isotonic

d. plyometric

 22. What is the Valsalva maneuver?

a. rapidly exhaling during a maximal muscular contraction

b. rapidly inhaling during a maximal muscular contraction

c. rapidly exhaling during a submaximal muscular contraction

d. breath-holding with a closed glottis

 23. Regarding the Valsalva maneuver, which of the following statements is *incorrect?*

a. It causes an increase in abdominal cavity pressure.

b. It causes an increase in thoracic cavity pressure.

c. It is caused by exerting force against a closed glottis.

d. It facilitates return of blood to the heart.

 24. What term best describes a type of muscle contraction in which the prime mover exerts force greater than resistance, resulting in muscle shortening and joint movement?

a. isometric

b. isokinetic

c. isotonic

d. plyometric

_B_ 25. Which term refers to a reduction in the size of a muscle or body part?

    a. accretion

    b. atrophy

    c. hyperplasia

    d. hypertrophy

_D_ 26. Which term refers to an increase in the size of a muscle or other body part caused by cell enlargement?

    a. accretion

    b. atrophy

    c. hyperplasia

    d. hypertrophy

_D_ 27. Which term refers to the eccentric loading of a muscle just prior to concentric muscular contraction?

    a. isometric

    b. isotonic

    c. isokinetic

    d. plyometric

_D_ 28. What is quantified by the RPE scale?

    a. degree of difficulty in breathing during exercise

    b. degree of chest pain during exercise

    c. degree of light-headedness during exercise

    d. subjective feeling of physical effort during exercise

_E_ 29. The RPE scale allows the exerciser to report subjective feelings during exercise taking what into consideration?

    a. general fatigue

    b. environmental conditions

    c. individual fitness level

    d. *a* and *b*

    e. *a*, *b*, and *c*

_E_ 30. What did the original RPE scale (6-20 points) take into consideration?

    a. blood lactic acid accumulation

    b. HR during exercise

    c. linear increase in O_2 consumption

    d. *a* and *b*

    e. *b* and *c*

X _D_ 31. Using the original RPE scale (6-20 points), what level of perceived exertion is associated with a CRF training effect?

_C_

    a. 6-9 points

    b. 10-12 points

    c. 13-16 points

    d. none of the above

_D_ 32. What is the predicted maximal HR (beats per minute) for a 37-year-old male?

    a. 153

    b. 163

    c. 173

    d. 183

_B_ 33. Bob is a 42-year-old, active nonsmoker who has received physician clearance to take part in a CRF exercise program. According to ACSM guidelines, what is the range of Bob's exercise intensity (beats per minute), based on a percentage of HR max?

    a. 71-107

    b. 107-160

    c. 110-130

    d. 150-180

_____ 34. Beth is a 52-year-old, active nonsmoker who has received physician clearance to participate in a CRF exercise program. Beth's resting HR is 72 beats per minute, and during a GXT her HR max was determined to be 168 beats per minute. Based on ACSM guidelines, what would be Beth's exercise intensity (beats per minute) as measured by the HRR method?

a. 105-125

b. 110-130

c. 120-154

d. 135-180

35. What is the predicted maximal HR range in beats per minute for 68 percent of the population for individuals who are 27 years of age?

a. 172-192

b. 181-205

c. 195-210

d. 211-220

36. Jim's maximum HR is 189 beats per minute while his prone and standing resting HRs are 62 and 75 beats per minute, respectively. What would be Jim's target HR range (beats per minute) as calculated by the HRR method?

a. 126-170

b. 132-172

c. 140-180

d. 149-189

37. Which of the following is (are) true regarding the RPE scale?

a. It is unreliable in approximately 30 percent of the population.

b. It is useful for monitoring exercise intensity in individuals who have difficulty palpating HR.

c. It is not recommended if the exercise participant's HR response is known to be altered because of a change in medication.

d. a and b

e. b and c

38. When monitoring exercise HR at the carotid artery, how should the participant palpate the carotid artery?

    a. Use the thumb to apply moderate pressure.

    b. Use the index and middle fingers to apply heavy pressure.

    c. Use the thumb and index finger to apply light pressure.

    d. Use the index and middle fingers to apply light pressure.

39. Which of the following signs and symptoms of excessive effort may appear during or immediately following exercise?

    a. ataxia

    b. dyspnea lasting for more than 10 minutes

    c. decrease in SBP

    d. *b* and *c*

    e. *a, b, c,* and *d*

40. Which of the following physical markers is (are) associated with overtraining?

    a. decrease in performance

    b. increase in maximal O_2 uptake

    c. altered HR and BP

    d. *a* and *c*

    e. *b* and *c*

41. How is exercise intensity best monitored during pregnancy?

    a. palpating HR at the radial artery

    b. palpating HR at the brachial artery

    c. using the RPE scale

    d. using a dyspnea scale

42. During pregnancy, which activity should be avoided after the first trimester?

    a. any exercise in the supine position

    b. any exercise in the prone position

    c. cycling

    d. swimming

C 43. What aerobic intensity range and resistance training would be included in an appropriate exercise program for individuals diagnosed with hypertension?

    a. 40-70 percent and a resistance-training component consisting of both high repetitions/low resistance and isometric activities

    b. 40-70 percent and a resistance-training component consisting of moderate isometric activities

    c. 40-70 percent and a resistance-training component consisting of high repetitions and low resistance

    d. 75-85 percent and a resistance-training component consisting of low repetitions and high resistance

    e. 80-90 percent and a resistance-training component consisting of high repetitions and low resistance

X D 44. How should the duration of exercise be modified for an
B   obese individual?

    a. Limit duration to 20 minutes.

    b. Keep calorie expenditure to 200-300 kcal per session.

    c. Keep caloric expenditure to 500-600 kcal per session.

    d. Keep caloric expenditure to 3,000-3,600 kcal/week.

    e. c and d

C 45. Which of the following activities would be most appropriate for an individual who experiences exercise-induced asthma?

    a. brisk walking in cold weather

    b. jogging in cold weather

    c. swimming

    d. a and b

D 46. What are the proper adjustments when one is using the Nautilus leg extension machine?

    a. Place arms across the chest, adjust seat so that roller pad contacts the middle of the shin, and align knees with axis of machine.

b. Place arms across the chest, adjust seat so that roller pad contacts shin slightly above the ankles, and align knees with axis of machine.

c. Grasp handles on each side of seat, align knees with axis of machine, and lean forward as knees are fully extended.

d. Grasp handles on each side of seat, align knees with axis of machine, and keep back flat against back pad as knees are fully extended.

47. When spotting the supine dumbbell fly, where should the spotter's hands be positioned?

a. under or on the performer's elbows

b. under or on the performer's wrist

c. on the dumbbells

d. no spotter needed for this exercise

48. Which of the following flexibility exercises is designed to stretch the deltoids and pectoralis major?

a. behind-the-neck stretch (chicken wing)

b. pretzel

c. seated lean-back

d. yoga plow

49. When are the force demands greatest during execution of a bent-knee sit-up with respect to the position of the hands and arms?

a. straight above the head with straight elbows

b. behind the head with elbows bent and fingers inter-woven

c. across the chest with hands touching opposite shoulders

d. on the thighs or beside the body

50. Which resistance exercise primarily trains the biceps brachii?

a. hammer curl

b. overhead elbow extension

c. knee flexion

d. knee extension

X <u>D</u> 51. Which of the following best describes the resistance-training system known as an ascending pyramid?

A

    a. performing multiple sets, starting at about 10-12 repetitions and systematically increasing resistance over several sets until only 1 repetition is possible

    b. performing multiple sets starting at 1RM and systematically reducing resistance and increasing repetitions until 10-12 repetitions are completed

    c. performing one set of several exercises in succession for the same muscle group, each building upon the other with no rest between exercises

    d. *a* and *b*

    e. none of the above

<u>D</u> 52. Performing 12 biceps curls immediately followed by 12 repetitions of triceps extensions is an example of what resistance-training system?

    a. plyometrics

    b. pyramiding

    c. split routine

    d. super sets

<u>B</u> 53. Depth jumping is an example of which of the following?

    a. pyramiding

    b. plyometrics

    c. super sets

    d. split routine

X <u>C</u> 54. Which apparatus is known for its isokinetic qualities?

A

    a. Cybex

    b. Air-dyne

    c. free weights

    d. Lifesteps

X <u>B</u> 55. Isotonic exercises are primarily performed on which type of resistance-training equipment?

D

    a. constant resistance–free weights

b. variable resistance–Nautilus

c. Biodex

d. *a* and *b*

e. *b* and *c*

56. Which of the following type of aerobic exercise equipment would be most appropriate for an obese individual?

a. step bench for high-impact aerobics

b. bicycle

c. jump rope

d. treadmill for running

57. What is (are) the potential disadvantage(s) of using a stair climber for an aerobic workout?

a. It may aggravate some knee conditions.

b. It requires an element of coordination and balance.

c. Beginning performers tend to bend too far forward while leaning on the handrails.

d. *a* and *c*

e. *a, b,* and *c*

58. Extreme hyperflexion of the neck is associated with which of the following exercises?

a. neck bridge

b. neck circles

c. plough

d. *a* and *b*

59. What potential risk is associated with the standing straight-leg toe touch?

a. excessive flexion forces on the cervical vertebrae

b. excessive extension forces on the cervical vertebrae

c. excessive flexion forces on the lumbar and sacral vertebrae

d. none of the above

_B_ 60. What method of training is a compromise between aerobic exercise and muscular strength/endurance training?

    a. continuous

    b. circuit

    c. interval

    d. pyramid resistance

_B_ 61. What characterizes an interval training program?

    a. alternating bouts of low-intensity exercise followed by a recovery period

    b. alternating bouts of high-intensity exercise followed by a recovery period

    c. ability to tax the aerobic pathway

    d. *a* and *c*

_B_ 62. Which of the following is a style (method) of teaching in which cognitive learning is increased and problem solving is encouraged?

    a. direct

    b. indirect

    c. modified direct

    d. part-whole

X _D_ 63. Which of the following is a style (method) of teaching that
    A   is effective for organizing large-group exercise sessions?

    a. direct

    b. indirect

    c. modified indirect

    d. part-whole

_D_ 64. As an exercise leader, which of the following organizational patterns would allow you to systemically observe clients during an exercise session without requiring excessive movement on your part?

    a. positioning yourself in the middle of the gym

    b. walking slowly around the perimeter of the gym

    c. positioning yourself at one end of the gym

    d. positioning yourself at one station and rotating clients through all stations

65. During an exercise session it is important that the exercise leader see all clients and be seen by all clients. How can this goal best be accomplished?

    a. walking around the perimeter of the class

    b. walking around and through the class

    c. positioning yourself at the front of the class

    d. positioning yourself in the middle of the class

66. When communicating with clients who have been placed in a circle formation, you should do which of the following?

    a. Stand outside of the circle.

    b. Stand in the middle of the circle.

    c. Become a member of the circle.

    d. Never use a circle formation when communicating with clients.

67. What common mistake(s) is (are) made by exercise professionals when attempting to communicate with a client?

    a. paying too much attention to nonverbal communication

    b. failing to recognize how the client interpreted the verbal message

    c. failing to recognize the role of voice quality (loudness, pitch) in conveying the intended message

    d. *a* and *b*

    e. *b* and *c*

68. When the exercise professional verbally communicates with a client, approximately what should the physical distance between the two be?

    a. 1/2 to 1 1/2 feet

    b. 4 to 12 feet

    c. 15 to 20 feet

    d. 21 to 25 feet

_E_ 69. Exercises performed in water are especially beneficial for which of the following?

a. obese individuals

b. pregnant women

c. arthritic patients

d. *a* and *c*

e. *a, b,* and *c*

_A_ 70. How can one increase the exercise intensity experienced during water exercise?

D

a. by exercising in deeper water

b. by exercising in shallow water

c. by jogging in a circle and quickly changing direction, thus being required to jog against the water current

d. *a* and *c*

e. *b* and *c*

_C_ 71. Which stretching technique is most likely to require the aid of an exercise partner?

a. ballistic

b. dynamic

c. proprioceptive neuromuscular facilitation

d. static

_C_ 72. To accommodate for different levels of abdominal strength/endurance within the same exercise class, what are the appropriate hand and arm positions for untrained and trained individuals when performing a bent-knee sit-up?

a. The untrained should place the hands and arms behind the head with elbows bent and fingers interwoven, while the trained should place the hands and arms across the chest.

b. The untrained should place the hands and arms across the chest, while the trained should position the hands and arms on the thighs.

c. The untrained should place the hands and arms beside the hips or on the thighs, while the trained should

position the hands and arms behind the head, being
careful not to hyperflex the neck.

d. Hand and arm position does not affect the intensity of
performing a bent-knee sit-up.

 73. How can different levels of physical fitness (intensity) be
accomplished within the same aerobic step-bench exercise
class?

a. choreographing different ranges of movement for the
different fitness levels

b. reducing or increasing exercise intensity by adjusting
the height of the step bench

c. choreographing step-bench routine to incorporate
high-impact exercises for the highly conditioned and
low-impact exercises for the less fit individuals

d. *a* and *b*

e. *a, b,* and *c*

 74. What are appropriate activities to be included in a low-
impact exercise class?

a. walking, jogging, cycling, swimming

b. walking, jumping jacks, cycling, swimming

c. walking, stepping up and down on an aerobic step
bench, jumping jacks, stair running

d. walking, stepping up and down on an aerobic step
bench, cycling, swimming

 75. What activities are most appropriate for an obese individual with bone or joint problems?

a. walking, jogging, jumping jacks

b. walking, swimming, cycling

c. walking, running stairs, use of stair climber

d. walking, running up and down an aerobic step bench

 76. What long-term benefits are associated with regular fitness
participation?

a. increased maximal O_2 uptake, higher myocardial O_2 cost
for a given workload, moderate reduction in BP for
hypertensive individuals

b. moderate reduction in BP for hypertensive individuals, lower myocardial O_2 cost for a given workload, increase in HDL-C

c. decreased threshold for the onset of disease symptoms (angina pectoris), large reduction in BP for hypertensive individuals

d. increased maximal O_2 uptake, lower myocardial O_2 cost for a given workload, moderate reduction in BP for hypertensive individuals, decrease in HDL-C

77. What frequency, duration, and intensity of exercise for individuals with controlled hypertension are suggested by the ACSM exercise prescription guidelines?

a. two to three days per week for 20-30 minutes per session at an intensity of 60-80 percent of maximal aerobic capacity

b. four to five days per week for 30-60 minutes per session at an intensity of 40-70 percent of maximal aerobic capacity

c. daily exercise for 60-90 minutes per session at an intensity of 60-80 percent of maximal aerobic capacity

d. daily exercise for 60-90 minutes per session at an intensity of 80-95 percent of maximal aerobic capacity

78. The duration of a CRF exercise session should balance exercise intensity so as to result in an energy expenditure of how many kilocalories per week from exercise?

a. 500-900

b. 1,000-2,000

c. 2,500-3,000

d. 3,500-4,000

79. What are the recommended frequency, intensity (HRR), and duration for maintaining CRF after 28-plus weeks of training?

a. three days per week, 60-70 percent HRR, 20 minutes

b. three days per week, 70-85 percent HRR, 30-45 minutes

c. four days per week, 40-50 percent HRR, 15 minutes

d. five days per week, 70-80 percent HRR, 60-90 minutes

80. Using METs as a means of monitoring exercise intensity is most appropriate for individuals who have which of the following?

   a. high functional capacity

   b. cardiac disease

   c. pulmonary disease

   d. METs should not be used to monitor exercise intensity in any population.

 81. Which resistance-training regimen is designed to emphasize muscular hypertrophy?

   a. high-intensity, low-volume training with brief rest periods between sets

   b. high-intensity, low-volume training with a full recovery rest period between sets

   c. moderate-intensity, high-volume training with brief to moderate rest periods between sets

   d. moderate-intensity, high-volume training with a full recovery rest period between sets

 82. What is proper procedure for performing the bench press?

   a. Lower the bar to touch the clavicle and place soles of feet on bench to reduce lower back curvature.

   b. Lower the bar to touch the chest near the nipples and place feet on the floor.

   c. Exhale when the bar is lowered and inhale when the bar is pushed upward.

   d. Arch the lower back in order to gain more force during the upward movement of the barbell.

 83. What procedures are correct when one uses the back hyperextension bench?

   a. Hang torso down to form a 45-degree angle at the hip joint before the torso is extended upward.

   b. Raise the trunk until the torso is parallel with the floor.

   c. Raise the trunk until the torso is at an angle greater than 180 degrees in relation to the thigh and legs.

   d. Raise the trunk, attempting to extend the hip joint as far as possible.

84. What should load assignment for a given resistance-training exercise be based on?

  a. a percentage of the established or estimated 1RM
  b. guesswork
  c. relative strength
  d. the participant's height and weight

 85. What time interval should be allowed between trials when one is attempting to establish a 1RM?

  a. one minute
  b. two to four minutes
  c. five minutes
  d. seven minutes

 86. How often should one stretch to *maintain* musculoskeletal flexibility?

  a. one day per week, holding each stretch for 5-10 seconds
  b. two days per week, holding each stretch for 10-15 seconds
  c. three days per week, holding each stretch for 10-30 seconds
  d. four days per month, holding each stretch for 60-90 seconds

 87. What is the correct procedure when one is reaching as far as possible while performing the sit-and-reach test?

  a. bouncing forward
  b. placing the head between the arms
  c. hyperextending the neck to view the measurement scale
  d. keeping both legs straight

 88. What is a disadvantage of interval training?

  a. It is psychologically demanding.
  b. It trains only the aerobic pathway.
  c. It is detrimental to hamstring flexibility.
  d. It is not a valuable training method for athletes in such popular sports as basketball and volleyball.

X A 89. Anaerobic work intervals of less than 30 seconds are gener-
   B   ally followed with a rest interval that is approximately how
          many times longer than the work interval?

   a. two

   b. three

   c. four

   d. five

   e. six

D 90. What is (are) the potential disadvantage(s) of some
       resistance-exercise machines?

   a. Adjustability may not accommodate both short and tall
      individuals.

   b. The machine may not simulate the type of activity in
      which an athletic is engaged (training specificity).

   c. Exercise machines are not capable of allowing for
      multiple-joint exercises.

   d. *a* and *b*

   e. *a* and *c*

D 91. What is an advantage of using dumbbells instead of a
       traditional Olympic barbell to perform a bench press?

   a. A complete set of dumbbells is cheaper than a 300-
      pound Olympic barbell set.

   b. Dumbbells are easier to balance.

   c. No spotter is needed with the use of dumbbells.

   d. Dumbbells allow for a greater ROM.

X C 92. Acclimatization to high altitude takes about how many
   B   weeks for altitudes up to 7,500 feet?

   a. one

   b. two

   c. three

   d. four

   e. five

__E__ 93. What changes are involved when one exercises at high altitude?

a. increased pulmonary ventilation

b. feeling of breathlessness

c. increased HR at rest and exercise

d. *a* and *b*

e. *a*, *b*, and *c*

__C__ 94. Which of the following modes of aerobic exercise would be most appropriate for an obese individual?

a. jogging on an outdoor track

b. jogging on an indoor carpet-covered track

c. water exercise

d. high-impact aerobic step class

__A__ 95. Which situation would require exercise placement in a supervised exercise program?

a. two major CAD risk factors

b. functional capacity of 8 METs

c. functional capacity of 10 METs

d. *a* and *b*

e. *a*, *b*, and *c*

__E__ 96. In which of the following is there the greatest need to periodically assess changes in physical fitness status?

a. individuals whose initial level of fitness was high

b. individuals whose initial level of fitness was low

c. individuals who have had a change in medication

d. *a* and *c*

e. *b* and *c*

REFERENCES FOR FURTHER STUDY

1. ACSM. (1991). *Certified News, 1* (2).

2. ACSM. (1993). *ACSM's resource manual for guidelines for exercise testing and prescription* (2nd ed.). Malvern, PA: Lea & Febiger.

3. ACSM. (1995). *ACSM's guidelines for exercise testing and prescription* (5th ed.). Baltimore: Williams & Wilkins.

4. Baechle, T.R. (Ed.). (1994). *Essentials of strength training and conditioning.* Champaign, IL: Human Kinetics.

5. Chu, D.A. (1992). *Jumping into plyometrics.* Champaign, IL: Human Kinetics.

6. Fleck, S.J., & Kraemer, W.J. (1997). *Designing resistance training programs* (2nd ed.). Champaign, IL: Human Kinetics.

7. Howley, E.T., & Franks, B.D. (1997). *Health fitness instructor's handbook* (3rd ed.). Champaign, IL: Human Kinetics.

8. McArdle, W.D., Katch, F.I., & Katch, V.L. (1991). *Exercise physiology: Energy, nutrition, and human performance* (3rd ed.). Philadelphia: Lea & Febiger.

ANSWERS

Question number	Answer	KSA number	Reference	Page number
1	b	1	3	156
2	e	1	3	158
3	e	1	3	163
4	d	1	3	166
5	c	2	3	4
6	d	3	4	448
7	b	3	3	169
8	b	3	3	169
9	c	3	3	170
10	a	4	4	405
11	c	4	7	293
12	a	4	4	406
13	a	5	4	289
14	c	6	2	384
15	d	6	2	383
16	a	6	4	259, 289

Question number	Answer	KSA number	Reference	Page number
17	c	7	3	174
18	d	7	3	174
		7	7	94
19	a	7	3	174
20	c	7	7	95
21	a	7	6	28
22	d	7	7	297
23	d	7	7	297
24	c	7	6	18
25	b	7	7	233
26	d	7	7	233
27	d	7	6	35
28	d	8	3	167
29	e	8	3	67
30	e	8	3	67
31	c	8	3	67
32	d	9	7	276
33	b	9	3	158
34	c	9	3	158, 160
35	b	9	3	129
36	b	9	3	160
37	b	10	3	160, 162
38	d	10	3	76
39	e	11	2	315
40	d	11	4	141
41	c	12	3	237
42	a	12	3	236

Question number	Answer	KSA number	Reference	Page number
43	c	12	3	210
44	b	12	3	212
45	c	12	7	365
46	d	13	4	375
47	b	13	4	348
48	c	14	4	300
49	a	15	4	36
50	a	16	4	359
51	a	17	6	124
52	d	17	6	127
53	b	17	5	5
54	a	18	6	45
55	d	18	7	297
56	b	19	3	212
57	e	19	2	345
58	c	20	1	2
59	c	20	1	3
60	b	21	4	411
61	b	21	4	78
62	b	22	2	321
63	a	22	2	321
64	d	23	2	322
65	b	23	2	322
66	c	23	2	323
67	e	24	2	319-320
68	b	24	2	320
69	e	25	3	212, 230, 236

Question number	Answer	KSA number	Reference	Page number
✕ 70	d	25	2	347
71	c	26	4	293
72	c	27	7	107
73	d	27	2	346
✕ 74	d	28	2	346
75	b	28	2	346
76	b	29	3	5
✕ 77	b	31	3	210
78	b	32	3	166
79	b	33	3	168
80	a	34	3	162
✕ 81	c	35	4	57
82	b	36	4	361-362
83	b	36	4	354
84	a	37	4	439
85	b	37	4	438
86	c	38	3	172
✕ 87	b	39	2	332
88	a	40	8	441
✕ 89	b	40	4	410
90	d	41	4	417
91	d	41	4	360
✕ 92	b	42	2	140
93	e	42	3	295
94	c	43	3	212
95	a	43	3	175
96	e	46	7	280

Nutrition
and Weight
Management

The objectives in this ACSM KSA category, Nutrition and Weight Management, are straightforward, and the readings and references we provide should prepare you adequately for the written examination, even without a special course in nutrition. Note that objective #21 requires you to demonstrate familiarity with several resource papers (ACSM, 1995, p. 329). These papers are listed at the end of this chapter in a special Suggested Readings section. We recommend that you obtain these papers and read them carefully. In light of the importance of these readings, we have put less emphasis on practice questions in this chapter. You will therefore be able to allot more of your study time for this part of the examination to working through the information in the readings. On the basis of previous ACSM Health/Fitness Instructor certification examinations, you are likely to receive approximately 15 questions from this category.

PRACTICE QUESTIONS

Directions: Each question is followed by either four or five possible answers. Select the *best* answer to the question.

 1. What is obesity?

 a. a condition in individuals who are 20-30 percent or more above the average weight for their size

b. a percent body fat of 25 (males) and 30 (females) or more

c. a BMI of >25 kg/m²

d. *a* and *b*

e. *a, b,* and *c*

 2. A man who weighs 180 pounds and is 70 inches tall would have a relative weight of 116.5 percent. This person is 16.5 percent above normal. What do you know about his weight?

a. He is at a desirable relative weight.

b. He is overweight.

c. He is mildly obese.

d. He is moderately obese.

e. He is severely obese.

3. What is lean body mass?

   a. fat-free mass, excluding essential fat

   b. the mass of the human body minus all storage fat

   c. body weight minus all body fat including essential body fat

   d. *a* and *b*

   e. *a, b,* and *c*

 4. What is the term for a serious condition, found most often among teenage girls, in which there is a loss of appetite and a possible progression to various degrees of emaciation?

   a. bulimia

   b. anorexia nervosa

   c. negative caloric balance

   d. android-type obesity

5. If one observed in a female athlete a weight loss or gain, excessive concern about weight, a visit to the bathroom after meals, depression, and/or severe criticism of her own body, which of the following conditions might be expected?

   a. anorexia nervosa

   b. anorexia athletica

   c. bulimia nervosa

   d. athletica bulimia

 6. In assessment of obesity as a possible health risk, more than ___ percent body fat should be considered. What term(s) below is (are) related to a high risk for cardiovascular disease and diabetes?

   a. regional body fat distribution

   b. android-type obesity

   c. gynoid-type obesity

   d. *a* and *b*

   e. *a, b,* and *c*

✗ C 7. Which of the following conditions may develop as a result
   of too much body fat?
   a. kidney disease; cirrhosis of the liver
   b. arthritis; cancer of the colon
   c. CAD; hypercholesteremia
   d. *a* and *b*
   e. *a, b,* and *c*

C 8. The most effective weight loss program would include
   which of the following?
   a. 500 kcal/day; less than 10 percent fat calories
   b. aerobic exercise; less than 500 kcal/day
   c. aerobic exercise; no less than 1,000 kcal/day
   d. anaerobic exercise; at least 1,000 kcal/day

D 9. Caloric restriction as the sole means of weight management
   is *not* recommended, for which of the following reasons?
   a. As much as 25 percent of the weight loss by dieting alone
      can be lean body mass.
   b. A rapid decline in resting metabolic rate is observed.
   c. Individuals become more anxious, and depression is
      more characteristic on this type of protocol.
   d. *a* and *b*
   e. *a, b,* and *c*

✗ 10. What is (are) true about rapid weight loss?
   a. It may occur during exercise.
   b. It is attributable to water loss.
   c. It is recommended for athletes attempting to make
      a particular weight category before an event (e.g.,
      wrestling).
   d. *a* and *b*
   e. *a, b,* and *c*

11. What is the best way to burn calories and lose body fat?

   a. Work at a lower percentage of $\dot{V}O_2$max (50 vs. 70 percent).

   b. Expend the most total calories possible within the time frame of the exercise session.

   c. Consume a very low calorie diet (e.g., < 500 kcal/day).

   d. *a* and *b*

   e. *a, b,* and *c*

12. Which of the following could be implemented in designing a sensible weight loss plan?

   a. a 3,500-kcal deficit in the weight management plan to lose 1 pound

   b. a deficit of 500 kcal/day over the week to lose 1 pound/ week

   c. negative caloric intake coupled with exercise

   d. *a* and *b*

   e. *a, b,* and *c*

13. Which of the mechanisms below is (are) thought to influence the hypothalamus in body weight management?

   a. enzymatic theory, which states that food intake is related to the regulation of enzymes controlling the metabolic pathways

   b. aminostatic theory, which states that food intake is related to blood enzyme levels

   c. glucostatic theory, which states that food intake is related to blood glucose levels

   d. lipostatic theory, which states that food intake is related to percent body fat

14. In which of the following are a fat-soluble vitamin and its associated functions correctly matched?

   a. vitamin A–facilitates blood clotting

   b. vitamin D–aids in growth and formation of bones and teeth

    c. vitamin E–is important for proper reproductive function in humans

    d. vitamin K–is essential in the prevention of night blindness

    e. *a* and *b*

15. Of the vitamins listed below, which is (are) correctly paired with its (their) symptoms of oversupplementation?

    a. ascorbic acid–diarrhea, kidney stones, rebound scurvy

    b. niacin–headaches, burning and itching skin, liver damage

    c. pyridoxine–no observable symptoms of excessive consumption observed with this vitamin

    d. *a* and *b*

    e. *a, b,* and *c*

16. Which set correctly matches the vitamin with its functions and possible toxicity symptoms?

    a. retinol–coenzyme in CHO metabolism–loss of nerve sensation

    b. thiamin–coenzyme in energy metabolism–no observable symptoms of excessive consumption

    c. cobalamin–maintenance of epithelial tissue–thrombosis

    d. pantothenic acid–a part of coenzyme A–diarrhea, possible kidney stones, and rebound scurvy

17. Which of the following is (are) true regarding salt tablets?

    a. They may be taken if the athlete loses substantial amounts of weight from sweat loss during exercise.

    b. They are not generally necessary to replace electrolytes under normal exercising conditions.

    c. They are recommended for anyone working outdoors.

    d. *a* and *b*

    e. *a, b,* and *c*

18. Which of the following is (are) true regarding diet pills?

    a. They consist of sympathomimetic amines or amphetamines.

b. They can cause elevation of HR and BP.

c. They alter exercise capacity and cause fatigue.

d. *a* and *b*

e. *a, b,* and *c*

19. A variety of nutritional aids advertise performance enhancement. For which of the following product(s) is the associated claim true?

a. chromium picolinate; increases muscle cell uptake of amino acids

b. caffeine; improves performance in endurance activities

c. amino acid tablets, protein powders; improve muscle mass gains

d. *a* and *b*

e. *a, b,* and *c*

20. Exercise capacity can be reduced by how small a percentage drop in body weight caused by sweating?

a. 1

b. 2

c. 3

d. 4

21. Which of the guidelines below should be observed when one considers fluid replacement drinks for a prolonged exercise event?

a. At least 180-240 milliliters of fluid should be consumed every 10-15 minutes.

b. The drink should contain 5 percent but no more than 10 percent CHO, so that the body is able to empty 1 liter of fluid from the stomach every hour.

c. The fluid should be cold for rapid stomach emptying.

d. *a* and *b*

e. *a, b,* and *c*

22. Listed below are statements characterizing the USDA Food Guide Pyramid. Which is true?

    a. Four food groups make up the Food Guide Pyramid.

    b. The majority of calories in the diet should come from (1) the bread, cereal, rice, and pasta group; (2) the vegetable group; and (3) the fruit group.

    c. Because dry beans are listed in the meat category, one should consume fewer beans in the diet.

    d. Fats and oils should be consumed only if one is lactose intolerant.

23. Of the following, which guideline is from the 1990 update of the "Dietary Guidelines for Americans"?

    a. Maintain a healthy body weight.

    b. Eat foods rich in Ca^{++} and iron.

    c. Avoid salt and sodium.

    d. Eat two or three eggs per week to maintain adequate protein levels.

24. Which of the following is (are) recommended to prevent bone loss in females?

    a. Women at high risk for osteoporosis should consume foods rich in Ca^{++}.

    b. Ca^{++} intake should be appropriate throughout life so that bone mass is optimal prior to adulthood.

    c. Women should participate in noncontact sports.

    d. *a* and *b*

    e. *a, b,* and *c*

25. What is (are) the major factor(s) associated with iron deficiency?

    a. inadequate dietary iron

    b. destruction of red blood cells via exercise

    c. bleeding from the gastrointestinal tract

    d. *a* and *b*

    e. *a, b,* and *c*

26. Increased levels of physical activity is (are) associated with which of the following blood lipid parameters?

    a. lower level of plasma triglycerides

    b. lower level of plasma low-density lipoproteins

    c. high level of plasma high-density lipoproteins

    d. *a* and *b*

    e. *a, b,* and *c*

27. Why might a modified-fat diet, along with physical activity, be beneficial in altering a less-than-optimal blood lipid profile?

    a. A low-fat diet will reduce TC.

    b. Exercise and diet together will offset possible decreases observed in high-density lipoproteins when diet alone is modified.

    c. An overall low-fat diet will increase dietary trans-fatty acid absorptions, which is recommended to decrease serum low-density lipoproteins and increase serum high-density lipoproteins.

    d. *a* and *b*

    e. *a, b,* and *c*

28. Which of the following lifestyle factors may have a beneficial effect on the blood lipid profile?

    a. aerobic exercise

    b. body leanness

    c. not smoking

    d. *a* and *b*

    e. *a, b,* and *c*

29. Reducing which of the following is most important in lowering LDL-C and TC?

    a. dietary cholesterol

    b. dietary saturated fats

    c. body weight

    d. dietary caffeine

30. One pound of fat is equivalent to how many kilocalories?
    a. 3,086
    b. 3,500
    c. 4,086
    d. 4,500

31. Which guidelines provide for the recommended weekly weight loss without compromising health?
    a. 1,200 kcal/day obtained from a variety of foods
    b. daily exercise with a caloric expenditure of a least 300 kcal per session
    c. a diet that includes foods that are appetizing, cost effective, and easy to prepare
    d. *a* and *b*
    e. *a*, *b*, and *c*

32. Which of the following is *not* correct regarding the essential nutrients?
    a. Protein is a primary source of energy.
    b. Vitamins are organic catalysts involved in metabolic reactions.
    c. Water is essential for life.
    d. Minerals form the greater portion of the hard parts of the body (e.g., bones, teeth, nails).

33. Which of the following is (are) true about CHOs?
    a. They are a basic source of energy for work.
    b. They are a crucial source of energy for red blood cells and neurons.
    c. They are implicated in the development of atherosclerosis.
    d. *a* and *b*
    e. *a*, *b*, and *c*

34. Which of the following is (are) true regarding water?
    a. It is an essential component of cell protoplasm.
    b. It is an important regulator of body temperature.

   c. It is essential for osmotic pressure maintenance.

   d. *a* and *b*

   e. *a*, *b*, and *c*

35. Which of the following is (are) true regarding proteins?

   a. They are a part of almost all enzymes in the body.

   b. When deaminated they provide a source of energy to the Krebs cycle.

   c. When in excess, they can be converted to glucose or fat.

   d. *a* and *b*

   e. *a*, *b*, and *c*

36. A female, interested in the proportion of grams of protein to be consumed in her diet, calculated the values below based on her body weight of 121 pounds. Which is correct?

   a. 59

   b. 56

   c. 50

   d. 44

37. Recommendations for dietary fat include (1) reducing the percentage of total calories from fat to a total of what percentage and (2) reducing the percentage of calories from saturated fat to what percentage, respectively?

   a. 40; 25

   b. 35; 20

   c. 30; 15

   d. 30; 10

38. Current information suggests that body fat distribution patterns may be associated with certain health risks. Which of the following is (are) true?

   a. Those with most of their body fat in the upper body are at risk for CAD.

   b. Android-type obesity poses greater health risks than gynoid-type obesity.

c. Clusters of symptoms known as "metabolic syndrome" are associated in those who carry their fat in the trunk and abdomen.

d. *a* and *b*

e. *a, b,* and *c*

39. Guidelines for caloric intake for an individual desiring to lose weight would include which of the following?

a. a deficit in calories to equal 1 percent of the total body weight per week

b. a caloric deficit to include not only a dietary deficit of calories, but also an increase in caloric expenditure via exercise (e.g., 300 kcal per session)

c. one day a week of complete fasting to cleanse the system of impurities

d. *a* and *b*

e. *a, b,* and *c*

40. An individual in your exercise program weighs 200 pounds and wishes to weigh 165 pounds. This person should do which of the following to lose the weight conservatively?

a. Reduce dietary intake by approximately 750-1,000 kcal daily.

b. Reduce dietary intake by approximately 450-700 kcal and increase energy expenditure via exercise by 300 kcal per session.

c. Have a gastric bypass and increase energy expenditure via exercise by 300 kcal per session.

d. Obtain a vertical band gastroplasty to "jump-start" the weight loss and proceed with an exercise program.

41. Which of the suggestions below could be part of a program for gaining weight?

a. Participate in a weight-training program.

b. Increase dietary caloric intake by 400 kcal/day.

c. Increase dietary protein by 14 grams/day via food.

d. *a* and *b*

e. *a, b,* and *c*

42. Of the following ergogenic aids, which could actually enhance performance?

a. bee pollen; improves metabolism and endurance performance

b. amino acid tablets; improve gains in muscle mass

c. ginseng; enhances energy

d. carbohydrate loading; aids in muscle glycogen sparing

43. Which of the following nutritional ergogenic aids is claimed to be effective for exercise tasks relying on the ATP-PC system and anaerobic glycolysis (e.g., exercise lasting one to four minutes)?

a. carbohydrate loading

b. soda loading

c. glucose polymer fluid replacement drinks

d. Gatorade

44. For the following nutritional ergogenic supplements, which of the associated claims is (are) true?

a. chromium boron; strengthens muscle tissue

b. pangamic acid; improves endurance performance

c. vitamin B_{15}; increases muscle cell uptake of amino acids

d. *a* and *b*

e. *a, b,* and *c*

45. What is (are) the risk(s) associated with the use of caffeine?

a. possible contribution to dehydration due to its diuretic effect

b. nervousness, headaches, and insomnia in those not habituated

c. heart arrhythmias in susceptible individuals

d. *a* and *b*

e. *a, b,* and *c*

D 46. Nutritional factors related to the female athlete triad syndrome include which of the following beliefs?

    a. Heavily exercising females do not eat enough to match their caloric expenditures.

    b. Heavily exercising females are usually anorexic.

    c. Heavily exercising females are usually bulimic.

    d. Low fat consumption in the diet of heavily exercising females will result in amenorrhea.

SUGGESTED READINGS

To help you demonstrate familiarity with the National Institute of Health Consensus Statement on health risks of obesity, the Nutrition for Physical Fitness Position Paper of the American Dietetic Association, and the ACSM Position Stand on proper and improper weight loss programs, we recommend the following references.

ACSM. (1990). *The official position papers of the American College of Sports Medicine.* Indianapolis: ACSM National Center.

Anonymous. (1985). Health implications of obesity. *National Institutes of Health Consensus Development Conference Statement.* [Review]. *National Institutes of Health Consensus Development Conference Statement, 5* (9), 1-7.

Anonymous. (1986). Consensus development summaries. Health implications of obesity. National Institutes of Health. *Connecticut Medicine, 50* (3), 171-186.

Burton, B.T., Foster, W.R., Hirsch, J., & Van Itallie, T.B. (1985). Health implications of obesity: An NIH consensus development conference. *International Journal of Obesity, 9* (3), 155-170; published erratum, *International Journal of Obesity 10* (1), 79.

Schulz, L.O. (1986). Obese, overweight, desirable, ideal: Where to draw the line in 1986? *Journal of the American Dietetic Association, 86* (12), 1702-1704.

REFERENCES FOR FURTHER STUDY

1. ACSM. (1991). *Guidelines for exercise testing and prescription* (4th ed.). Malvern, PA: Lea & Febiger.

2. ACSM. (1993). *ACSM's resource manual for guidelines for exercise testing and prescription* (2nd ed.). Malvern, PA: Lea & Febiger.

3. ACSM. (1995). *ACSM's guidelines for exercise testing and prescription* (5th ed.). Baltimore: Williams & Wilkins.

4. Howley, E.T., & Franks, B.D. (1997). *Health fitness instructor's handbook* (3rd ed.). Champaign, IL: Human Kinetics.

5. McArdle, W.D., Katch, F.I., & Katch, V.I. (1991). *Exercise physiology: Energy, nutrition, and human performance* (3rd ed.). Malvern, PA: Lea & Febiger.

6. Nieman, D.C. (1995). *Fitness and sports medicine: A health-related approach* (3rd ed.). Palo Alto, CA: Bull.

7. Powers, S.K., & Howley, E.T. (1997). *Exercise physiology: Theory and applications to fitness and performance* (3rd ed.). Madison, WI: Brown & Benchmark.

8. Williams, M.H. (1995). *Nutrition for fitness and sport* (4th ed.). Madison, WI: Brown & Benchmark.

ANSWERS

Question number	Answer	KSA number	Reference	Page number
1	e	21	8	284, 442
			3	59
2	b	1	8	279, 443
			4	179
3	d	1	8	280, 440
			4	167
4	b	1	8	293
			4	195
5	c	1	8	293
6	e	1	8	289
			4	167
			2	455
7	e	2	8	288
			4	167
8	c	3	8	336
9	d	3	2	458

Question number	Answer	KSA number	Reference	Page number
10	d	4	8	334
11	b	5	8	333
12	e	5	4	188
13	c	5	6	382
			7	341
			8	284
14	b	6	4	153
15	d	6	8	186
16	b	6	8	186
17	d	7	8	261
			2	479
18	d	7	2	214
19	d	7	6	278
			7	461
20	b	8	6	259
			8	254
21	e	8	4	161
			8	264
22	b	9	4	159
23	a	9	4	159
			7	319
24	d	10	8	216
			6	437
25	e	10	8	222
			4	156
			6	266

Question number	Answer	KSA number	Reference	Page number
26	e	11	4	159
			8	149
27	d	11	8	152
			6	336
28	e	11	6	341
29	b	11	6	341
30	b	13	8	302
31	e	14	1	115
			3	218
32	a	15	8	2
33	d	15	8	93
			7	327
34	e	15	8	243
35	e	15	8	163
36	d	16	4	152
37	d	16	4	152
38	e	17	6	141, 372
			8	288
39	d	18	6	388
			4	190
40	b	18	6	388
41	e	18	8	362
42	d	19	4	162
			8	11, 104, 265
			6	274
43	b	19	6	280

Question number	Answer	KSA number	Reference	Page number
			8	265
44	d	19	6	279
			8	11
45	e	19	6	280
			8	47, 152
46	a	20	4	163

CHAPTER 13

Program Administration and Management

© Photophile/Jose Carillo

This chapter contains practice questions to test your knowledge of the ACSM certification KSAs in the category titled Program Administration and Management. Since this area tends to be a weakness in most applicants, you should consider setting up an appointment with an administrator to discuss these KSAs further. Fewer questions have been given to you in this section for two reasons. First, this way you will have more time to meet with an administrator. Second, questions from this section often relate to topics from other KSA categories, so a broad knowledge of information from all 10 KSA categories is as important as practice questions specifically dealing with Program Administration and Management. On the basis of previous ACSM Health/Fitness Instructor certification examinations, you are likely to receive approximately 10 questions from this category.

PRACTICE QUESTIONS

> Directions: Each question is followed by either four or five possible answers. Select the *best* answer to the question.

1. Which of the following is (are) possible assignments for the Health/Fitness Instructor?
   a. supervisor of programs
   b. exercise leader and programmer
   c. health counselor to the clientele
   d. supervisor of preventive programs
   e. *a, b,* and *c*

2. Which of the following is (are) a responsibility of the Health/Fitness Instructor?
   a. reporting directly to the health/fitness facility supervisor
   b. developing exercise prescriptions and teaching classes
   c. conducting staff evaluations
   d. *a* and *b*
   e. *a, b,* and *c*

3. As part of a Health/Fitness Instructor's responsibilities, he or she must be able to administer fitness-related programs within established budgetary guidelines. Which of the following would satisfy this responsibility?

   a. careful selection of the testing and exercise equipment to meet the needs of the facility

   b. ordering supplies on the basis of an accurate inventory

   c. including all personnel in the budgetary process yearly

   d. *a* and *b*

   e. *a*, *b*, and *c*

 4. Which of the following is (are) an appropriate question for formulating a marketing plan for a health/fitness facility?

   a. What is the geographic area in which the facility will be run and what are the demographics of the clientele to be served?

   b. Will the clientele be composed of families, children, elderly persons, factory workers, students, etc.?

   c. How much profit can be made by the facility?

   d. *a* and *b*

   e. *a*, *b*, and *c*

 5. Which of the following is (are) a good example of advertising strategies?

   a. word of mouth and staff speaking engagements

   b. direct mail and print advertising

   c. free memberships

   d. *a* and *b*

   e. *a*, *b*, and *c*

 6. A medium-sized health/fitness facility wishes to implement a new smoking-cessation program for its local community. In what promotional activities might this facility engage to maximize response and be cost effective at the same time?

   a. placing an advertisement in the newspaper to announce the program and a free lecture that will describe it

b. placing a cutout discount coupon in the newspaper near the announcement of the new program and free lecture

c. providing for a public service announcement on one or more local radio stations to announce the new program and free lecture

d. *a* and *b*

e. *a, b,* and *c*

D 7. A successful sales approach in a health/fitness facility includes which of the following procedures?

a. creating a list of qualified potential customers who might be interested in purchasing any of the health/ fitness services offered at the facility

b. approaching the prospective client via a number of methods: direct mail, telephone call, face-to-face contact

c. presenting a sales pitch to the prospective client suggesting that if the client does not participate in this program, his/her health could decline and illness and a poor quality of life will eventually follow

d. *a* and *b*

e. *a, b,* and *c*

E 8. Which of the following is (are) suitable for closing a sale for a health/fitness facility service?

a. explanation of all final terms of the sale (program content and costs of the service)

b. provision of a contract for the prospective client with all explanations of services and obligations of each party in writing

c. specifications on the delivery site and dates of the services to be provided to the prospective client

d. a discussion of the schedule and method of payment for the services to be provided by the facility

e. *a, b, c,* and *d*

B 9. What documentation is required to demonstrate accountability in the event a fitness facility client were to have an accident or show other signs and symptoms of illness during an exercise session?

a. job training and experience

b. fitness test results and exercise prescription for the client

c. record of equipment usage

d. results from complete blood screening

 10. If a client showed signs or symptoms requiring a physician's care, a variety of potential liability problems might arise. To avoid this potential problem, which of the following should be included in a facility's documentation?

a. information indicating that safe exercise intensity was recommended

b. information indicating that clients were instructed about safety in an activity and about use of the equipment

c. information indicating that exercise sessions were supervised

d. *a* and *b*

e. *a*, *b*, and *c*

 11. What element(s) should be contained in an accident report form?

a. an explanation of the circumstances surrounding the incident

b. information on the first or emergency care that was given

c. assurance that the client carries medical insurance

d. *a* and *b*

e. *a*, *b*, and *c*

 12. Record and business forms should be designed with which of the following in mind?

a. simplifying the operations in the business office

b. clarifying instructions regarding purpose and the procedures to be followed

c. appealing to prospective clients and informing them that the employees of this facility will go to great lengths in making things "beautiful" for the customer

    d. *a* and *b*

    e. *a, b,* and *c*

E 13. Which of the following types of documentation would demonstrate a strong record-keeping program?

    a. documentation of adherence to the program; can be used to demonstrate program effectiveness

    b. documentation of adherence to the program; can be used to formulate a cost-benefit ratio for insurance adjustments

    c. individual records on exercise participation; provide motivation for the client and make ongoing assessments of progress easier

    d. *a* and *b*

    e. *a, b,* and *c*

D 14. Which of the following is (are) true regarding the exercise educational component in any health/fitness facility?

    a. Individuals can be instructed about the role of exercise in their lives.

    b. A client can understand more fully what individual test results mean.

    c. Information can be provided to develop a more effective exercise program for the individual.

    d. *a* and *b*

    e. *a, b,* and *c*

D 15. Before a health/fitness facility begins a program in weight control, how should educational aspects be addressed?

    a. A knowledge baseline should be assessed for all participants, as there may be a variety of misunderstandings about nutrition and exercise.

    b. An attitude assessment should be conducted to ascertain the individual's eating behaviors and the role of food and its influence on the individual's weight problem.

    c. Aversion therapy should be conducted for those who have had problems in the past losing weight.

  d. *a* and *b*

  e. *a, b,* and *c*

 16. Which of the following is (are) true about a budget?

  a. It is a major component of long-range planning.

  b. It is based on realistic estimates of income and expenditures.

  c. If written well it allows for little flexibility, and this will keep down cost overruns.

  d. *a* and *b*

  e. *a, b,* and *c*

17. For a Health/Fitness Instructor, a complete understanding of the management of the facility is important. In which of the following are the roles correctly matched with the duties?

  a. supervisor–supervise staff, supervise participants, hire staff, provide opportunities for staff development

  b. planner–understand the goals of the organization, provide programming that mirrors the overall program purposes

  c. educator–train program staff, set up and conduct weekly staff meetings

  d. *a* and *b*

  e. *a, b,* and *c*

18. What factor(s) should be examined in an assessment of member retention?

  a. personal attributes: self-motivation, belief in the benefit of exercise to health

  b. environmental factors: spouse support, peer support, cost/benefit analysis

  c. physical activity characteristics: intensity of activity, perceived effort

  d. *a* and *b*

  e. *a, b,* and *c*

REFERENCES FOR FURTHER STUDY

1. ACSM. (1993). *ACSM's resource manual for guidelines for exercise testing and prescription* (2nd ed.). Malvern, PA: Lea & Febiger.
2. Gerson, R.F. (1989). *Marketing health/fitness services.* Champaign, IL: Human Kinetics.
3. Howley, E.T., & Franks, B.D. (1997). *Health fitness instructor's handbook* (3rd ed.). Champaign, IL: Human Kinetics.
4. Patton, R.W., Corry, J.M., Gettman, L.R., & Graf, J.S. (1986). *Implementing health/fitness programs.* Champaign, IL: Human Kinetics.
5. Patton, R.W., Grantham, W.C., Gerson, R.F., & Gettman, L.R. (1989). *Developing and managing health/fitness facilities.* Champaign, IL: Human Kinetics.

ANSWERS

Question number	Answer	KSA number	Reference	Page number
1	e	1	5	179
2	d	1	5	175
3	e	2	3	465, 469
4	d	3	2	5
			5	237
5	e	3	1	520
6	e	3	2	76
7	d	4	2	103
8	e	4	5	257
9	b	5	1	522
10	e	5	5	283
11	d	6	5	284
12	d	6	5	272
13	e	6	4	218
14	d	7	4	94
15	d	7	4	107
16	d	8	3	465
17	e	8	4	74
18	d	8	3	333

CHAPTER 14

Solving Metabolic Equations

Along with questions from each of the 10 ACSM KSA categories, one block of questions in the written portion of the ACSM Health/Fitness Instructor certification examination will require you to solve basic metabolic equations. Therefore the purpose of this chapter is to present a brief tutorial to the potential certification candidate. In this tutorial you will learn how to systematically solve metabolic equations.

At the ACSM Health/Fitness Instructor level of certification, you will be required to calculate energy cost in both METs and kilocalories when mode of exercise includes any of the following: treadmill walking, treadmill running, leg and arm ergometry, and bench stepping (see KSA category, Exercise Physiology, objective #18, p. 310, ACSM, 1995). Table 14.1 summarizes the five metabolic equations that you will be required to use. While at first glance the metabolic equations may appear intimidating, with practice you will not only

Table 14.1   Metabolic Equations
Oxygen consumption = horizontal component   + vertical component + resting component

Treadmill walking (1.9-3.7 mph) = m/min × 0.1 ml O_2/kg/min
      + %grade/100 × m/min
      × 1.8 ml O_2/kg/min + 3.5 ml O_2/kg/min

Treadmill running (> 5 mph) = m/min × 0.2 ml O_2/kg/min
      + %grade/100 × m/min
      × 0.9 ml O_2/kg/min + 3.5 ml O_2/kg/min

Leg cycle ergometry (300-1,200 kgm/min) = 0 + *kgm/min
      × 2 ml O_2/kgm +
      3.5 ml O_2/kg/min × BW(kg)

Arm cycle ergometry (150-759 kgm/min) = 0 + **kgm/min × 3
      + 3.5 ml O_2/kg/min
      × BW(kg)

Bench stepping = steps/min × 0.35 ml O_2/kg/min + m/step
      × steps/min × 1.33 × 1.8
      + 0 (already part of horizontal and vertical component)

*kgm/min = kg (or kp) × flywheel distance in meters × pedal rate; kg = the resistance set on the ergometer; flywheel distance is a function of the ergometer brand (Monark = 6 m/rev; BodyGuard and Tunturi = 3 m/rev).

**kgm/min = kg of resistance on the arm crank × crank revolutions in meters × cranking rate in rev/min.

Data from Zigon, 1990.

feel your anxiety dissipating but will also learn to enjoy the challenge that this important task offers. On the basis of previous ACSM Health/Fitness Instructor certification examinations, you are likely to receive approximately 10 questions that will require you to mathematically solve a metabolic equation.

A SYSTEMATIC APPROACH FOR SOLVING METABOLIC EQUATIONS

As you can see in table 14.1, each metabolic equation, regardless of mode of activity, is composed of three common components. These are energy expenditure or O_2 consumption required of work performed (1) horizontally, (2) vertically, and (3) at rest. In view of this three-component model, your task will be to extract important information from a descriptive statement (the question), substitute these "knowns" into the appropriate metabolic equation, and then, using principles of elementary algebra, solve for the "unknown." The following is a list of the steps you should follow mathematically when solving any metabolic equation. It's extremely important to resist the temptation to take shortcuts; instead, get into the habit of following each and every step in this systematic approach. This approach will greatly reduce your chance of committing a silly error.

1. Read the descriptive statement (question) and identify important known information that you will need to substitute into a metabolic equation.
2. On a sheet of paper, write the knowns on the left side and the unknowns on the right side.
3. Select the appropriate metabolic equation.
4. Examine the available information to determine whether or not it is in the appropriate unit of measure. For example, you may be given treadmill speed (miles per hour) whereas the appropriate metabolic equation requires you to convert speed to meters per minute.
5. Using substitution, lay out the appropriate metabolic equation and solve for the unknown component.
6. Once you have solved for the unknown component, double-check to see that the answer is in the correct unit of measure and is reasonable.

IMPORTANT FACTS TO MEMORIZE

Initially, potential certification candidates worry needlessly about their ability to memorize all five metabolic equations. Rest assured that memorization of the metabolic equations is not essential. As part of your examination packet, you will receive a copy of the metabolic equations as they appear on pages 278-281 of *ACSM's Guidelines for Exercise Testing and Prescription* (ACSM, 1995). Nevertheless, while memorization is not essential, it is to your advantage to be so familiar with the equations that you do not have to constantly consult the handout. Remember, as we pointed out in chapter 2, you will be under a time constraint, and constantly referring to the metabolic equations handout can quickly eat up valuable time. By solving the problems presented in this chapter you will gradually become increasingly familiar with the structure of each equation. However, there is some information that will not be supplied to you on the exam. Therefore, you must simply put this information to memory. This essential information is presented in table 14.2.

SOLVING METABOLIC EQUATIONS

In this section we provide examples that show you how to solve each of the five types of metabolic equations. You should note that in some instances you solve for O_2 consumption ($\dot{V}O_2$) and energy expenditure (kilocalories), while in other instances you will be given this information and asked to calculate treadmill speed, treadmill grade, cycle ergometer resistance, or some other variable. How do you know when to report O_2 cost in absolute (ml/min) or relative (ml/kg/min) terms? If the activity is weight-bearing (walking, jogging/running, bench stepping), report $\dot{V}O_2$ in ml/kg/min. If the activity is non-weight-bearing (leg and arm cycle ergometry), report $\dot{V}O_2$ in ml/min.

In the following presentation of questions and solutions, we employ the systematic approach to solving metabolic equations. Each question is answered using the step-by-step format just explained, and items numbered 1-4 or 1-5 after each question correspond to these steps. Steps 1-4 are used if substitution is not necessary, and steps 1-5 are used if substitution (step 5) is necessary. This method may seem repetitive, but it encourages you to attack these difficult

Table 14.2 Facts for Memory	
Parameter	**Conversion factor**
Distance	1 in. = 2.54 cm
Speed	1 mph = 26.8 m/min
	walking = 1.9-3.7 mph
	running = > 5 mph
Power	1 watt = 6.12 kgm/min (round off to 6.0 for calculations)
	50 watts = 300 kgm/min
	1 MET = 3.5 ml O_2/kg/min
	1 kp = 1 kg
Weight	1 kg = 2.2 lb
Kilocalories	1 L O_2 = 5 kcal

questions in a consistent manner. This will increase your chances of success with metabolic calculations.

TREADMILL WALKING

Walking occurs between 50 and 100 m/min (1.9-3.7 mph). No formulas exist for speeds between 3.7 mph (walking) and 5.0 mph (jogging). If an individual is walking/jogging between 3.7 and 5.0 mph, you must use caution in deciding which equation to use. When there is no vertical component, as in level treadmill walking, for example, the vertical component equals zero. This is a weight-bearing activity. Oxygen cost is reported in relative terms, ml O_2/kg/min.

Practice Question 1

What is the relative O_2 consumption of walking at 3.0 mph up a 2% grade? Answer: 14.43 ml O_2/kg/min.

1. Read the question and identify important known information.

2. Write the knowns on the left side and the unknowns on the right side.

Known: Unknown:

grade = 2% $\dot{V}O_2$(relative)

speed = 3.0 mph

3. Select the appropriate metabolic equation (walking).

   $\dot{V}O_2$ = horizontal + vertical + resting

   To determine the horizontal, vertical, and resting components of this equation, use the following equalities:

   $\dot{V}O_2$(horizontal) = m/min $\times$ 0.1 ml O_2/kg/min

   $\dot{V}O_2$(vertical) = grade (as a fraction) $\times$ m/min
   $\times$ 1.8 ml O_2/kg/min

   $\dot{V}O_2$(resting) = 3.5 ml O_2/kg/min

4. Examine the available information. This problem requires you to convert miles per hour to meters per minute.

   Convert 3.0 mph to meters per minute.

   26.8 m/min $\times$ 3.0 mph = 80.4 m/min

5. Using the information from above, solve for the unknowns.

   a. $\dot{V}O_2$(horizontal) = m/min $\times$ 0.1 ml O_2/kg/min
      = 80.4 m/min $\times$ 0.1 ml O_2/kg/min
      = 8.04 ml O_2/kg/min

   b. $\dot{V}O_2$(vertical) = grade (as a fraction) $\times$ 1.8 ml O_2/kg/min
      = 0.02 $\times$ 80.4 m/min $\times$ 1.8 ml O_2/kg/min
      = 2.89 ml O_2/kg/min

   c. $\dot{V}O_2$(relative) = 8.04 ml O_2/kg/min + 2.89 ml O_2/kg/min
      + 3.5 ml O_2/kg/min

   d. $\dot{V}O_2$(relative) = 14.43 ml O_2/kg/min

Practice Question 2

An individual has set the treadmill at a 4% grade and 3.0 mph. Would a person wishing to exercise at approximately 5.0 METs be able to do so using these criteria? Answer: 17.33 ml O_2/kg/min; yes.

1. Read the question and identify important known information.

2. Write the knowns on the left side and the unknowns on the right side.

Known: Unknown:

grade = 4% or 0.04 $\dot{V}O_2$ (relative)

speed = 3.0 mph   Exercise criteria met to
                                work at 5.0 METs?

3. Select the appropriate metabolic equation (walking).

   $\dot{V}O_2$ = horizontal + vertical + resting

   To determine the horizontal, vertical, and resting components of this equation, use the following equalities:

   $\dot{V}O_2$(horizontal) = m/min × 0.1 ml O_2/kg/min

   $\dot{V}O_2$(vertical) = grade (as a fraction) × m/min
   × 1.8 ml O_2/kg/min

   $\dot{V}O_2$(resting) = 3.5 ml O_2/kg/min

   1 MET = 3.5 ml O_2/kg/min

4. Examine the available information. This problem requires you to convert miles per hour to meters per minute.

   Convert 3.0 mph to meters per minute.

   26.8 m/min × 3.0 mph = 80.4 m/min

5. Using the information from above, solve for the unknowns.

   a. $\dot{V}O_2$(horizontal) = m/min × 0.1 ml O_2/kg/min
      = 80.4 m/min × 0.1 ml O_2/kg/min
      = 8.04 ml O_2/kg/min

   b. $\dot{V}O_2$(vertical) = grade (as a fraction) × m/min
      × 1.8 ml O_2/kg/min
      = 0.04 × 80.4 m/min × 1.8 ml O_2/kg/min
      = 5.79 ml O_2/kg/min

   c. $\dot{V}O_2$(relative) = 8.04 ml O_2/kg/min + 5.79 ml O_2/kg/min
      + 3.5 ml O_2/kg/min

   d. $\dot{V}O_2$(relative) = 17.33 ml O_2/kg/min

   e. Is this person working at approximately 5.0 METs?

      $\dot{V}O_2$(relative) = 17.33 ml O_2/kg/min

      17.33 ml O_2/kg/min / 3.5 ml O_2/kg/min = 4.95 METs

   Answer: yes.

Practice Question 3

A cardiac patient was told by her doctor *not* to exercise any harder than 5 METs. At what speed (miles per hour) should this person walk if the grade is 5%? Answer: 2.85 mph.

1. Read the question and identify important known information.

2. Write the knowns on the left side and the unknowns on the right side.

Known:	Unknown:
grade = 5% or 0.05	$\dot{V}O_2$(relative)
METs = 5.0	speed

3. Select the appropriate metabolic equation (walking).

   $\dot{V}O_2$(relative) = horizontal + vertical + resting

   To determine the horizontal, vertical, and resting components of this equation, use the following equalities:

   $\dot{V}O_2$(horizontal) = m/min × 0.1 ml O_2/kg/min

   $\dot{V}O_2$(vertical) = grade (as a fraction) × m/min × 1.8 ml O_2/kg/min

   $\dot{V}O_2$(resting) = 3.5 ml O_2/kg/min

   1 MET = 3.5 ml O_2/kg/min

4. Examine the available information. This problem requires you to convert METs to $\dot{V}O_2$.

   Convert METs to $\dot{V}O_2$.

   5.0 × 3.5 ml O_2/kg/min = 17.5 ml O_2/kg/min (round off to 18.0)

5. Using the available information from above, solve for the unknowns.

   a. $\dot{V}O_2$(horizontal) = speed × 26.8 m/min × (0.1 ml O_2/kg/min)

   = speed × 2.68 ml O_2/kg/min

   b. $\dot{V}O_2$(vertical) = %grade (fraction) × m/min × 1.8 ml O_2/kg/min × speed

   = 0.05 × speed × 26.8 m/min × 1.8 ml O_2/kg/min

   = (speed) × 2.4 ml O_2/kg/min

c. $\dot{V}O_2$(relative) = 18.0 ml O_2/kg/min

18.0 ml/kg/min = (speed) $\times$ 2.68 ml O_2/kg/min + (speed)
$\times$ 2.4 ml O_2/kg/min + 3.5 ml O_2/kg/min
= (speed)5.09 + 3.5 ml O_2/kg/min

14.5 ml O_2/kg/min = (speed)5.09

Answer: speed = 2.85 mph.

TREADMILL RUNNING

Jogging or running occurs at speeds greater than 5.0 mph. Because this is a weight-bearing activity, O_2 cost is reported in relative terms, ml O_2/kg/min.

Practice Question 1

What is the O_2 cost of running on a treadmill at a speed of 6.0 mph and 8% grade? Answer: 47.24 ml O_2/kg/min.

1. Read the question and identify important known information.

2. Write the knowns on the left side and the unknowns on the right side.

Known:	Unknown:
grade = 8.0%	$\dot{V}O_2$(relative)
speed = 6.0 mph	

3. Select the appropriate metabolic equations (running).

   $\dot{V}O_2$ = horizontal + vertical + resting

   To determine the horizontal, vertical, and resting components of this equation, use the following equalities:

   $\dot{V}O_2$(horizontal) = m/min $\times$ 0.2 ml O_2/kg/min

   $\dot{V}O_2$(vertical) = grade (fraction) $\times$ m/min $\times$ .9 ml O_2/kg/min

   $\dot{V}O_2$(resting) = 3.5 ml O_2/kg/min

4. Examine the available information. This problem requires you to convert miles per hour to meters per minute.

   Convert miles per hour to meters per minute.

   26.8 m/min $\times$ 6.0 mph = 160.8 m/min

5. Using the information from above, solve for the unknowns.

a. $\dot{V}O_2(\text{horizontal}) = \text{m/min} \times 0.2 \text{ ml } O_2/\text{kg/min}$
$= 160.8 \text{ m/min} \times 0.2 \text{ ml } O_2/\text{kg/min}$
$= 32.16 \text{ ml } O_2/\text{kg/min}$

b. $\dot{V}O_2(\text{vertical}) = \text{grade (fraction)} \times \text{m/min} \times 0.9 \text{ ml } O_2/\text{kg/min}$
$= 0.08 \times 160.8 \text{ m/min} \times 0.9 \text{ ml } O_2/\text{kg/min}$
$= 11.58 \text{ ml } O_2/\text{kg/min}$

c. $\dot{V}O_2(\text{relative}) = 32.16 \text{ ml } O_2/\text{kg/min} + 11.58 \text{ ml } O_2/\text{kg/min}$
$+ 3.5 \text{ ml } O_2/\text{kg/min}$

d. $\dot{V}O_2(\text{relative}) = 47.24 \text{ ml } O_2/\text{kg/min}$

Practice Question 2

At what percent grade should the treadmill be set when a person wishes to exercise at 6 mph and 12 METs? Answer: 4%.

1. Read the question and identify important information.

2. Write the knowns on the left side and unknowns on the right side.

Known:	Unknown:
speed = 6 mph	$\dot{V}O_2(\text{relative})$
METs = 12.0	%grade

3. Select the appropriate metabolic equations (running).

$\dot{V}O_2 = \text{horizontal} + \text{vertical} + \text{resting}$

To determine the horizontal, vertical, and resting components of this equation, use the following equalities:

$\dot{V}O_2(\text{horizontal}) = \text{m/min} \times 0.2 \text{ ml } O_2/\text{kg/min}$
$\dot{V}O_2(\text{vertical}) = \text{grade (fraction)} \times \text{m/min} \times 0.9 \text{ ml } O_2/\text{kg/min}$
$\dot{V}O_2(\text{resting}) = 3.5 \text{ ml } O_2/\text{kg/min}$
$1 \text{ MET} = 3.5 \text{ ml } O_2/\text{kg/min}$

4. Examine the available information. This problem requires you to convert METs to $\dot{V}O_2(\text{relative})$ and miles per hour to meters per minute.

a. Convert METs to $\dot{V}O_2$(relative).

   12.0×3.5 ml O_2/kg/min = 42.0 ml O_2/kg/min

b. Convert 6 mph to meters per minute.

   26.8×6.0 mph = 160.8 m/min

5. Using the information from above, solve for the unknowns.

   a. $\dot{V}O_2$(horizontal) = 160.8 m/min $\times$ 0.2 ml O_2/kg/min

      = 32.16 ml O_2/kg/min

   b. $\dot{V}O_2$(vertical) = %grade $\times$ 160.8 m/min $\times$ 0.9 ml O_2/kg/min

      = (%grade) $\times$ 144.72 ml O_2/kg/min

   c. $\dot{V}O_2$(relative) = 32.16 ml O_2/kg/min
      + (%grade)144.72 ml O_2/kg/min
      + 3.5 ml O_2/kg/min

   d. 42.0 ml/kg/min = 35.66 ml O_2/kg/min
      + (%grade)144.72 ml O_2/kg/min

   6.34 ml/kg/min = (%grade)144.72 ml O_2/kg/min

   %grade = .044 or 4%

LEG CYCLE ERGOMETRY

Cycle ergometry is a non-weight-bearing activity, so $\dot{V}O_2$ is reported in absolute terms (L/min). $\dot{V}O_2$ can be estimated for work rates between 300 and 1,200 kgm (50-200 watts). There is no horizontal component in leg cycle ergometry because the bike is stationary. The vertical component is called a resistive component, and it equals the load (force in kilograms or kiloponds) at which the ergometer is set, times the flywheel circumference, times the number of pedal revolutions per minute. The flywheel on a Monark cycle ergometer travels at 6 m/rev; the flywheel on both the Tunturi and BodyGuard cycle ergometers travels at 3 m/rev. Pedal revolutions are monitored with a metronome. Pedal revolutions of 50-60 are ˙appropriate for untrained cyclists. For example, if you were pedaling at 50 rev/min on a Monark cycle ergometer, the distance traveled would equal 6 m/rev $\times$ 50 rev/min or 300 m/min. If a 1-kilogram force is set on the wheel, then 1 kilogram $\times$ 300 m/min = 300 kgm/min.

Practice Question 1

A 143-pound male pedals a Monark cycle ergometer at 50 rev/min against a resistance of 2.0 kilograms. What is the power

output? What is the relative $\dot{V}O_2$? How long would it take this individual to expend 500 kcal? Answer: 600 kgm/min; 21.96 ml O_2/kg/min; 70 min.

1. Read the question and identify important known information.

2. Write the knowns on the left side and the unknowns on the right side.

Known:	Unknown:
BW = 143 pounds	power
= 65 kilograms	vertical/resistive com-
rev/min = 50	ponent
force = 2 kilograms	$\dot{V}O_2$(relative)
flywheel circumference	time to expend 500 kcal
= 6 m/rev	

3. Select the appropriate metabolic equations (leg cycling).

$$\dot{V}O_2\text{(absolute)} = \text{vertical} + \text{resting}$$

To determine the vertical and resting components of this equation, use the following equalities:

$$\dot{V}O_2\text{(vertical)} = \text{kgm/min} \times 2 \text{ ml } O_2/\text{kgm}$$
$$\dot{V}O_2\text{(resting)} = 3.5 \text{ ml } O_2/\text{kg/min} \times \text{BW (in kilograms)}$$

4. Examine the available information. This problem requires you to determine the distance traveled and POWER output.

   a. Equations: distance = rev/min $\times$ m/rev; $P = (F \times d)/t$

   b. Solve for distance.

   distance = 50 rev/min $\times$ 6 m/rev
   $$= 300 \text{ m/min}$$

5. Using the information from above, solve for the remaining unknowns.

   a. Solve for POWER.

   Note that distance is expressed as a rate. So if we multiply the rate (300 m/min) times the force (2 kilograms) we will be able to calculate the power output [$P = (F \times d)/t$].

   POWER = 2 kilograms $\times$ 300 m/min

   Therefore, POWER output = 600 kgm/min

b. $\dot{V}O_2$(vertical) = kgm/min × 2 ml O_2/kgm

      = 600 kgm/min × 2 ml/kgm

      = 1,200 ml O_2/min

c. $\dot{V}O_2$(resting) = 3.5 ml O_2/kg/min × BW (in kilograms)

      = 3.5 ml O_2/kg/min × 65 kg

      = 227.5 ml O_2/min

d. $\dot{V}O_2$(absolute) = vertical + resting

      = 1,200 ml O_2/min + 227.5 ml O_2/min

      = 1427.5 ml O_2/min

If we want the relative O_2 cost of this cycle activity, we divide the absolute O_2 cost by the body weight in kilograms. Therefore, 1427.5 ml O_2/min / 65 kilograms = 21.96 ml/kg/min. Therefore, the relative $\dot{V}O_2$ = 21.96 ml/kg/min.

e. Time to expend 500 kcal?

Convert ml O_2/min to liters per minute.

  1427.5 ml O_2/min = 1.428 L O_2/min

  1.428 L O_2/min × 5 kcal/L = 7.14 kcal/min

  500 kcal/7.14 kcal/min = 70.03 min

Therefore, it would take 70 minutes to expend 500 kcal.

ARM CYCLE ERGOMETRY

Oxygen consumption can be estimated for arm cycle ergometry for work rates between 150 and 750 kgm/min (25-125 watts). Because this is a non-weight-bearing activity, relative O_2 consumption values must be converted to absolute terms (e.g., ml O_2/min or L O_2/min). As in leg cycle ergometry, there is no horizontal component.

Practice Question 1

A 50-kilogram female exercises on an arm cycle ergometer at 50 rev/min against a force of 25 watts. What is the absolute $\dot{V}O_2$ (ml O_2/min)? Answer: 625 ml O_2/min.

1. Read the question and identify important known information.

2. Write the knowns on the left side and the unknowns on the right side.

Known: Unknown:

BW = 50 kilograms $\dot{V}O_2$(absolute)

rev/min = 50

power = 25 watts

3. Select the appropriate metabolic equation (arm cycling).

$\dot{V}O_2$(absolute) = vertical + resting

To determine the vertical and resting components of this equation, use the following equalities:

$\dot{V}O_2$(vertical) = kgm/min × 3.0 ml O_2/kgm

$\dot{V}O_2$(resting) = 3.5 ml O_2/kg/min × BW (in kilograms)

4. Examine the available information. This problem requires you to convert watts to kgm/min.

Convert watts to kgm/min.

1 watt = 6 kgm/min

25 × 6 kgm/min = 150 kgm/min

25 watts = 150 kgm/min

Therefore, power output = 150 kgm/min

5. Using the information from above, solve for the remaining unknowns.

a. $\dot{V}O_2$(vertical) = kgm/min × 3.0 ml/kgm

= 150 kgm/min × 3.0 ml/kgm

= 450 ml O_2/min

b. $\dot{V}O_2$(resting) = 3.5 ml O_2/kg/min × BW in kilograms

= 3.5 ml O_2/kg/min × 50 kg

= 175 ml O_2/min

c. $\dot{V}O_2$(absolute) = resistive + resting

= 450 ml O_2/min + 175 ml O_2/min

= 625 ml O_2/min

Therefore, the absolute $\dot{V}O_2$ for this arm cycle exercise is 625 ml O_2/min.

BENCH STEPPING

Bench stepping is a weight-bearing activity requiring the use of relative $\dot{V}O_2$. The resting component (equals 0) is already determined as part of the horizontal and vertical components. The step or bench height must be converted to meters. The constant, 1.33, is used in bench-stepping exercise as it includes both the positive component of stepping up (1.0) and the negative component of stepping down (0.33).

Practice Question 1

What is the O$_2$ cost of bench stepping when the height of the bench is 8 inches and the stepping rate is 20? Answer: 16.73 ml O$_2$/kg/min.

1. Read the question and identify important known information.

2. Write the knowns on the left side and the unknowns on the right side.

   Known: Unknown:

   bench height = 8 inches $\dot{V}O_2$(relative)

   step rate = 20 steps per minute

3. Select the appropriate metabolic equations (bench stepping).

   $$\dot{V}O_2(\text{relative}) = \dot{V}O_2(\text{horizontal}) + \dot{V}O_2(\text{vertical})$$

   To determine the horizontal and vertical components of this equation, use the following equalities:

   $$\dot{V}O_2(\text{horizontal}) = \text{steps/min} \times .35 \text{ ml } O_2/\text{kg/min}$$
   $$\dot{V}O_2(\text{vertical}) = \text{m/step} \times \text{steps/min} \times 1.33 \times 1.8$$

4. Examine the available information. This problem requires you to convert the bench step height in inches to meters.

   Convert bench step height in inches to meters.

   8 inches $\times$ 0.0254 meters = .2032 meters

5. Using the information from above, solve for the remaining unknowns.

   a. $\dot{V}O_2(\text{horizontal})$ = steps/min $\times$ 0.35 ml O$_2$/kg/min

      = 20 steps/min $\times$ 0.35 ml O$_2$/kg/min

      = 7 ml O$_2$/kg/min

b. $\dot{V}O_2$(vertical) = .2032 m/step $\times$ 20 steps/min $\times$ 1.33 $\times$ 1.8
   = 9.73 ml O_2/kg/min

c. $\dot{V}O_2$(relative) = 7.0 ml O_2/kg/min + 9.73 ml O_2/kg/min
   = 16.73 ml O_2/kg/min

PRACTICING METABOLIC CALCULATIONS

The following are 25 metabolic calculations. Work through them using the systematic approach and following the format of the examples you have seen.

1. What is the $\dot{V}O_2$ cost of exercising on a treadmill at 2.5 mph and a 6% grade?

2. What is the MET requirement and what is the caloric expenditure for an exercise session on the treadmill if you weigh 75 kilograms and want to exercise by walking at 3.7 mph up a 10% grade?

3. A cardiac patient cannot walk any faster than 2 mph, but has been told that she must exercise at 8 METs. At what percent grade should the treadmill be set?

4. An elderly lady who weighs 142 pounds exercises on her treadmill at 2.5 mph. What is her caloric expenditure for a 20-minute exercise session?

5. A male who weighs 200 pounds wishes to lose weight. If he exercises on the treadmill at 3.0 mph and 10% grade, how long will it take to expend enough calories to equal approximately 1 pound?

6. If a 75-kilogram man runs at 9 mph for 30 minutes, how many kilocalories will he expend?

7. What is the O_2 cost of running at 10 mph up a 10% grade on a treadmill?

8. At what grade should you exercise on a treadmill if you wish to work at a 13 MET capacity? Treadmill speed is 6 mph.

9. What is the caloric cost (per minute) of the treadmill exercise in question #7? The person performing this activity weighs 55 kilograms.

10. What would be the O_2 cost of running on the level at 8 mph?

11. What is the O_2 cost of leg cycle ergometry when the workload is 400 watts and body weight is 65 kilograms?

12. What is the energy cost in METs if a person is cycling at a work rate of 300 kgm/min and weighs 50 kilograms?

13. What is the workload in watts if a person is pedaling at 60 rev/min at a resistance of 2 kiloponds on a Monark ergometer?

14. What is the absolute O_2 cost of cycling at 150 watts on a Monark cycle when the person weighs 175 pounds?

15. How long would the person in question #14 have to exercise in order to expend 400 kcal?

16. What is the cost in METs for a 125-pound woman who exercises at 125 watts on an arm cycle ergometer?

17. What is the O_2 cost of arm cranking at 125 watts when you weigh 80 kilograms?

18. What is the total energy expenditure for the person in question #17 after exercising for 30 minutes?

19. A man is cranking at 50 watts on the arm crank ergometer. What is his MET level? BW = 84 kg

20. A woman who weighs 95 kilograms reached 125 watts on an arm-cranking test before fatiguing. She wishes to train at 70 percent of her maximal capacity. At what work rate should she train on the arm crank ergometer?

21. What is the O_2 cost of bench stepping at a rate of 20 steps per minute when the bench is 8 inches high?

22. For a 60-kilogram woman exercising on a 30-centimeter bench at a rate of 40 steps per minute, what would be the relative O_2 cost and energy expenditure in METs?

23. What is the total energy expenditure for the woman in question #22 after she has exercised for five minutes?

24. You have a client who needs preliminary testing. Your facility uses bench stepping to assess initial fitness level (bench = 6 inches; protocol uses 15 steps per minute). If your client had been told by his doctor to exercise, but *not* above 6 METs initially, could you test your client with your current protocol?

25. An individual wants to start a stair-stepping exercise routine at home. The steps are 7 inches high. What stepping rate should he use if he wishes to exercise at 6 METs?

REFERENCES FOR FURTHER STUDY

ACSM. (1995). *ACSM's guidelines for exercise testing and prescription* (5th ed.). Baltimore: Williams & Wilkins.

Flood, D.K. (1996). *Practical math for health fitness professionals.* Champaign, IL: Human Kinetics.

Zigon, S.T. (1990). *How to use the American College of Sports Medicine metabolic equations.* Canton, OH: Professional Reports Corporation.

ANSWERS

1. 17.44 ml O_2/kg/min
2. 8.93 METs; 11 kcal/min
3. 20%
4. 65 kcal in 20 minutes
5. approximately 5 hours
6. 582 kcal in 30 minutes
7. 81.22 ml O_2/kg/min
8. .068 or 7%
9. 22.34 kcal/min
10. 46.38 ml O_2/kg/min
11. 5027.5 ml O_2/min
12. 4.4 METs
13. 120 watts
14. 2078 ml O_2/min
15. 38.46 minutes
16. 12.34 METs
17. $2,530$ ml O_2/min
18. 379.5 kcal for 30 minutes
19. 4.06 METs
20. 525 kgm/min or 87.5 watts
21. 16.58 ml O_2/kg/min
22. 42.73 ml O_2/kg/min; 12 METs
23. 64.10 kcal for five minutes
24. Yes, protocol requires 3 METs
25. Approximately 27 steps per minute

CHAPTER 15

Analyzing Case Studies

© Terry Wild Studio

Most of the study questions you have seen so far have been presented in a straightforward manner. You have simply been asked to respond to specific questions in à multiple-choice format. However, when working in a real-world setting, the exercise professional must learn to make decisions based on an array of information. This information is generally obtained through such means as medical history, blood profile analyses, physical examination, and exercise test results. Collectively this information is referred to as a case study. Your job as an exercise professional is to consider all available information in making your exercise recommendations. These are some of the questions that the exercise professional may be asking when analyzing the information in a client's file:

- What is the client's risk stratification?
- Does the client exhibit major signs or symptoms suggestive of cardiopulmonary or metabolic disease?
- Are blood chemistry profiles in line with suggested recommendations?
- Did the client exhibit a normal HR and BP response to exercise?
- What is the client's true functional capacity? How does this information impact upon establishing a target HR range?
- Should the client be placed in a supervised or an unsupervised program?
- Does the client exhibit any orthopedic or other exercise-related limitations?
- What would be the most appropriate mode of exercise for this client?

In this chapter you will have the opportunity to review four case studies. We suggest that after studying each case file, you attempt to formulate your own series of important questions before answering the questions we have supplied. If you would like additional practice in analyzing case studies, consult the work of Wasserman and colleagues (1987).

CASE STUDY 1

Paul is a male who is 36 years of age, weighs 88 kilograms, is 178 centimeters tall, and has 28 percent body fat. Blood chemistry values indicated that TC = 270 mg · dl^{-1} and HDL-C = 38 mg · dl^{-1}. Paul's mother died of a heart attack at the age of 63, and his father had a heart attack at the age of 68. Paul is sedentary and has engaged in no endurance-training program since college. Table 15.1 shows the results of his maximal GXT, conducted by his physician.

_____ 1. What is the range of Paul's target HR, in beats per minute, based on 60-80 percent $\dot{V}O_2$max?

    a. 122-135

    b. 135-152

    c. 139-168

    d. 158-177

_____ 2. Paul's target HR range as calculated in problem #1 corresponds to what work-rate range in METs?

    a. 1.5; 3.5

    b. 2.5; 5.0

    c. 6.3; 8.4

    d. 8.6; 9.5

_____ 3. What is revealed by Paul's medical history and blood profile?

    a. a positive family history for CAD

Table 15.1 Test: Balke, 3 mi · hr^{-1}, 2.5% per 2 min

Grade %	METs	SBP	DBP	HR	ECG	Symptoms
	Rest	126	88	70	—	—
2.5	4.3	142	86	142	—	—
5	5.4	148	88	150	—	—
7.5	6.4	162	86	160	—	—
10	7.4	174	84	168	—	—
12.5	8.5	186	84	176	—	—
15	9.5	194	84	190	—	Calf tight
17.5	10.5	198	84	198	—	Fatigue

Reprinted from Howley and Franks, 1997.

      b. a significantly elevated HDL-C value

      c. an HDL-C level that is below the minimal recommendation

      d. a TC:HDL-C ratio of 7.1

___ 4. What is revealed by Paul's GXT results?

      a. a true functional capacity of 9.5 METs

      b. a true functional capacity of 10.5 METs

      c. an elevated resting BP

      d. an abnormal DBP response during exercise

CASE STUDY 2

Mary is a 38-year-old female who is 170 centimeters tall, weighs 61.4 kilograms, and has 39 percent body fat. Blood chemistry values indicate a TC of 188 mg · dl^{-1} and an HDL-C of 59 mg · dl^{-1}. Her resting BP is 124/80. Family history indicates that her father suffered a nonfatal heart attack at the age of 67. Mary has smoked one pack of cigarettes a day for the past 13 years. The results of her submaximal cycle ergometer test are shown in table 15.2.

___ 5. What does Mary's blood lipid profile indicate?

      a. a TC:HDL-C ratio of approximately 4.1

      b. a high HDL-C value

      c. an elevated TC value

      d. *b* and *c*

      e. none of the above

Table 15.2 Test: Y Way of Fitness		
Work rate (kgm · min^{-1})	HR (Min 2)	HR (Min 3)
150	118	120
300	134	136

Note. Pedal rate = 50 rpm; predicted HR max = 182 beats · min^{-1}; seat height = 6; 85% HR max = 155 beats · min^{-1}.

Reprinted from Howley and Franks, 1997.

___ 6. Mary wishes to reduce her percentage of body fat to 22. What would be her corresponding target body weight?

    a. 50 kilograms

    b. 55 kilograms

    c. 121 pounds

    d. 130 pounds

___ 7. What is revealed by Mary's medical history?

    a. a positive health history for the development of CAD

    b. a need to participate in a smoking-cessation program

    c. a need to elevate her HDL-C

    d. a need to lower TC

CASE STUDY 3

Chris is a female, 49 years of age, who is 164 centimeters tall, weighs 93 kilograms, and has 40 percent body fat. Her serum TC is 190 mg · dl^{-1}, serum triglycerides are 100 mg · dl^{-1}, blood glucose is 92 mg · dl^{-1}, and resting BP is 130/84. In college she was active in swimming and tennis, but since then she has had a relatively sedentary lifestyle. Her goal is to lose weight and become active again. Table 15.3 shows the results of a submaximal GXT taken to 85 percent of predicted maximal HR.

___ 8. What is the most appropriate mode of activity for Chris given that she wants to become more active and lose weight?

    a. a sport such as basketball, which she enjoys

Table 15.3	Test: Balke, 3 mi · hr^{-1}, 2.5% per 2 min				
Grade (%)	METs	SBP (mm Hg)	DBP (mm Hg)	HR	RPE
2.5	4.3	134	90	122	11
5	5.4	140	90	132	13
7.5	6.4	162	80	143	14

Note. Predicted HR max = 171 beats · min^{-1} and 85% HR max = 145 beats · min^{-1}.

Reprinted from Howley and Franks, 1992.

   b. walking and/or swimming

   c. jogging

   d. high-impact aerobic stepping

___ 9. What is revealed by information from Chris's case file?

   a. It is likely that she is a diabetic.

   b. She has an elevated serum triglyceride level.

   c. She has a TC:HDL-C ratio of 1.9.

   d. She exhibited normal HR, BP, and RPE response during exercise.

CASE STUDY 4

A 28-year-old female police officer (5 feet 5 inches, 140 pounds, 28 percent body fat) has enrolled in the adult fitness program. Her job demands a fairly high level of physical fitness, a level she was able to achieve six years ago when she passed the physical fitness test battery used by the police department.

Before becoming a police officer, the client jogged 20 minutes usually three times a week. Since starting this job, she has had little or no time for exercise and has gained 15 pounds. She works eight hours a day, is divorced, and takes care of two children, ages 7 and 9.

At least three times a week, she and the children dine out, usually at fast-foot restaurants like Kentucky Fried Chicken, Burger King, or Taco Bell. She reports that her job, along with the sole responsibility for raising her children, is quite stressful. Occasionally she experiences headaches and a tightness in the back of her neck. Usually in the evening she has one glass of wine to relax.

Her medical history reveals that she smoked one pack of cigarettes a day for four years while she was in college. She quit smoking three years ago. For the past two years she has tried some quick weight-loss diets, with little success. She was hospitalized two times to give birth to her children. She reports that her grandfather died of heart disease when he was 62 and that her older brother has high BP.

Recently the client had her blood chemistry analyzed because she was feeling light-headed and dizzy after eating. In an attempt to lose weight she eats only one large meal a day, at dinnertime. Results of the blood analysis were TC = 220 mg · dl⁻¹; triglycerides = 98 mg · dl⁻¹; glucose = 82 mg · dl⁻¹; HDL = 37 mg · dl⁻¹; and TC:HDL ratio = 5.9.

The exercise evaluation yielded the data in the following list and in table 15.4:

Mode/Protocol: Treadmill/Modified Bruce

Resting data: Heart rate = 75 bpm

BP = 140/82 mm Hg

____ 10. What is the number of major CAD risk factors present in this client's CAD risk profile?

    a. none

    b. one

    c. two

    d. three

    e. four

____ 11. What is this client's initial risk stratification?

    a. apparently healthy–older

    b. apparently healthy–younger

    c. increased risk

    d. known disease

Table 15.4 Data Accumulated During Case Study 4

Stage (METs)	Workload (min)	Duration (beats/min)	HR	BP (mm Hg)	RPE
1	2.3	3	126	145/78	8
2	3.5	3	142	160/78	11
3	4.6	3	165	172/80	14
4	7.0	3	190	189/82	18

Endpoint: Stage 4 (2.5 mph, 12% grade). Terminated because of fatigue. No significant ST-segment depression or arrhythmias.

Reprinted from Heyward, 1991.

___ 12. Which of the following is *not* an independent positive CAD risk factor?

    a. family history

    b. hypercholesterolemia

    c. diabetes mellitus

    d. obesity

___ 13. What is revealed by this client's GXT results?

    a. a functional aerobic capacity of approximately 24.5 ml · kg · min^{-1}

    b. an abnormal DBP response to exercise

    c. a abnormal SBP response between stage 3 and stage 4 of the GXT

    d. none of the above

___ 14. If this client were to participate in an outdoor walking program, on a level track, at a training intensity of 60 percent of VO$_2$ max, what would be her walking speed?

    a. 11 minutes 22 seconds/mile

    b. 12 minutes 44 seconds/mile

    c. 14 minutes 16 seconds/mile

    d. 15 minutes 32 seconds/mile

REFERENCES FOR FURTHER STUDY

1. Heyward, V.H. (1991). *Advanced fitness assessment and exercise prescription* (2nd ed.). Champaign, IL: Human Kinetics.

2. Howley, E.T., & Franks, B.D. (1992). *Health fitness instructor's handbook* (2nd ed.). Champaign, IL: Human Kinetics.

3. Howley, E.T., & Franks, B.D. (1997). *Health fitness instructor's handbook* (3rd ed.). Champaign, IL: Human Kinetics.

4. Wasserman, K., Kansen, J.E., Sue, D.Y., & Whipp, B.J. (1987). *Principles of exercise testing and interpretation.* Philadelphia: Lea & Febiger.

ANSWERS

Question number	Answer	Reference	Page number
1	d	3	478
2	c	3	478
3	d	3	42
4	b	3	288
5	e	3	478
6	b	3	478
7	b	3	478
8	b	2	253
9	d	2	253
10	c	1	279
11	c	1	279
12	d	1	279
13	a	1	279-280
14	c	1	281

The Practice Examination

In appendix A, we provide you with a practice written examination. We encourage you to take this practice examination during one three-hour sitting. This process will allow you to become familiar with, and thus prepare you for, the feelings you are likely to experience during the actual certification examination.

In appendix B on page 259 you will find an answer sheet for the practice exam. Enter the appropriate answer for each question in the first blank line next to the question number. Use the second column of blank lines for correcting your practice examination. Fill in the correct answer for each question you answered incorrectly. This will make it easy for you to determine the areas in which you need to improve.

Two sets of answers are furnished at the end of the practice examination. The first set is a sequential answer list (#1-#103), while the second provides answers broken down by KSA category. This second answer set will allow you to better identify categories of strength and weakness. You should strive to obtain at least 80 percent in each of the KSA categories before attempting ACSM certification (even though ACSM standards for passing are lower).

ACSM HEALTH/FITNESS INSTRUCTOR PRACTICE EXAMINATION

Directions: Each question is followed by either four or five possible answers. Select the *best* answer to the question.

1. What is the correct order of muscle contraction events?

   a. nerve impulse generated; Ca^{++} released from the sarco-plasmic reticulum; actin and myosin coupled to form acto-myosin; $ATP \rightarrow ADP + Pi + ENERGY$

   b. nerve impulse generated; $ATP \rightarrow ADP + Pi + ENERGY$; actin and myosin coupled to form actomyosin; Ca^{++} released from the sarcoplasmic reticulum

   c. nerve impulse generated; $ATP \rightarrow ADP + Pi + ENERGY$; Ca^{++} released from the sarcoplasmic reticulum; actin and myosin coupled to form actomyosin

   d. nerve impulse generated; actin and myosin coupled to form actomyosin; $ATP \rightarrow ADP + Pi + ENERGY$; Ca^{++} released from the sarcoplasmic reticulum

2. What is the immediate source of energy for muscular work?

   a. ATP-PC system

   b. anaerobic glycolysis

   c. aerobic glycolysis

   d. oxidative phosphorylation

3. Why is children's ability to thermoregulate during heat exposure less efficient than that of adults?

   a. Children have a higher threshold for the onset of sweating, a higher skin blood flow, a higher sweat output rate from heat-activated sweat glands, and a larger surface area to body mass ratio.

   b. Children have a higher threshold for the onset of sweating, a lower skin blood flow, a lower sweat output rate from heat-activated sweat glands, and a larger surface area to body mass ratio.

   c. Children have a lower threshold for the onset of sweating, a lower skin blood flow, a higher sweat output rate from heat-activated sweat glands, and a smaller surface area to body mass ratio.

   d. Children have a lower threshold for the onset of sweating, a higher skin blood flow, a lower sweat output rate from heat-activated sweat glands, and a smaller surface area to body mass ratio.

4. How should the exercise professional deal with a participant who overexerts him/herself during an exercise session?

   a. Recognize the potential liability that this person presents to the program and immediately drop the participant from the program.

   b. Explain to the participant the potential dangers associated with exercising above one's target HR.

   c. Suspend the participant's exercise facility privileges for one week.

   d. Assign a staff member to exercise with this individual on a full-time basis to ensure that the participant will not over-exert him/herself.

   e. *b* and *d*

5. What directions should the exercise professional give to a participant who is about to perform the sit-and-reach test?

   a. Bounce, to reach farther on the measurement scale.

   b. Remove shoes prior to testing.

   c. Perform two trials, to provide two scores that will be re-corded as an average.

   d. Inhale and drop the head between the arms when reaching forward.

   e. *b* and *d*

6. Which of the following is (are) a negative CAD risk factor(s)?

   a. hypertension

   b. diabetes

   c. high serum HDL-C

   d. *a* and *b*

7. What must be included in the emergency plan for a health/fitness facility?

   a. provisions for physical access to all areas of the facility, including a plan to treat bystanders in an emergency

   b. provisions for documenting all activities

   c. a telephone in every room

    d. *a* and *b*

    e. *a*, *b*, and *c*

8. Which of the following is *not* generally a psychological sign associated with overtraining?

    a. anxiety

    b. irritability

    c. confusion

    d. increased vigor

9. What is the average percentage of body fat for males and females, respectively, and what are the recommended values for males and females, respectively?

    a. 10-12 percent, 18-20 percent; 5-10 percent, 10-12 percent

    b. 12-15 percent, 20-23 percent; 10-12 percent, 12-15 percent

    c. 15-18 percent, 22-25 percent; 12-18 percent, 16-25 percent

    d. 18-20 percent, 25-28 percent; 16-20 percent, 23-25 percent

10. What role in administration and program management does the Health/Fitness Instructor have?

    a. scheduling fitness programs and staff to conduct classes

    b. developing variety with respect to fitness classes

    c. training new staff members

    d. *a* and *b*

    e. *a*, *b*, and *c*

11. Which of the following muscles adducts, medially rotates, and extends the arm?

    a. latissimus dorsi

    b. infraspinatus

    c. pectoralis major

    d. triceps brachii

12. What supplies ATP during long-term (10-60 minute) exercise?

    a. aerobic metabolism of CHO

    b. aerobic metabolism of fat

c. aerobic metabolism of fat and CHO

d. aerobic metabolism of protein

13. Which of the following is true with regard to HR in an elderly population?

a. It tends to decline, and maximal HR tends to decrease.

b. It tends to increase, and maximal HR increases in men but decreases in women.

c. It shows little to no change, and maximal HR tends to decrease.

d. It increases in women but decreases in men, and maximal HR tends to decrease in both men and women.

14. Which of the following is considered the most effective method for changing health behaviors?

a. goal-setting

b. reinforcement

c. shaping

d. stimulus-control

15. What directions should the exercise professional give to a male participant for executing the push-up endurance test?

a. Perform as many push-ups as possible within one minute.

b. Perform as many push-ups as possible without resting–no time limit.

c. Lower the chest until it contacts the instructor's fist, which is placed on the floor.

d. *a* and *c*

e. *b* and *c*

16. Individuals with diabetes mellitus should be classified as patients with disease in all but which of the following cases?

a. an insulin-dependent diabetic who is more than 30 years of age

b. a non-insulin-dependent diabetic who is more than 35 years of age

   c. a person who is 25 years of age and has been an insulin-dependent diabetic since the age of 15 years

   d. a person who is 33 years of age and has been an insulin-dependent diabetic since the age of 17 years

17. First aid for a contusion, strain, or sprain should *not* include which of the following?

   a. rest

   b. compression

   c. 20-30-minute applications of heat

   d. referral to a physician if function is impaired

18. What is the recommended exercise intensity for individuals more than 65 years of age?

   a. 50-70 percent of HR max

   b. 50-70 percent of HRR

   c. 75-80 percent of HR max

   d. 75-80 percent of HRR

19. Which of the following obesity classifications is associated with CAD and diabetes?

   a. android-type obesity

   b. gynoid-type obesity

   c. morbid obesity

   d. lipostatic obesity

20. For an exercise professional, what is the first step in working with an apparently healthy 35-year-old male who is interested in beginning a low- to moderate-intensity exercise program?

   a. administering the Physical Activity Readiness Questionnaire

   b. asking a client to obtain a physician's clearance before beginning a program

   c. contacting the individual's cardiologist to obtain permission for GXT

   d. giving the Cooper 12-minute run test

21. Which muscles flex the forearm?
    a. the biceps brachii
    b. the brachialis
    c. the brachioradialis
    d. *a* and *b*
    e. *a*, *b*, and *c*

22. What term is given to the amount of blood pumped out of the heart with every beat?
    a. stroke volume
    b. ejection fraction
    c. end-systolic volume
    d. cardiac output

23. Which of the following is true regarding children and training?
    a. Excessive endurance exercise could place a prepubescent child at increased risk for a decrease in height.
    b. Children should *not* be permitted to perform maximum lifts (1RM) until reaching a Tanner stage 3 level of maturity.
    c. Prepubescent children who regularly participate in a weight-training program generally demonstrate increased strength with moderate muscle hypertrophy.
    d. ACSM guidelines recommend that young children perform resistance-training exercise no more than two days per week.

24. To enhance exercise adherence, what should the exercise professional communicate to the exercise participant?
    a. the need to continue exercising even when not feeling well, since even one missed exercise session can lead to long-term noncompliance
    b. the need to develop a relapse-prevention strategy prior to the start of the exercise program
    c. the appropriateness of a sense of guilt after missing an exercise session
    d. the need to realize that after missing an exercise session, it will be necessary to work twice as hard in the next session in order to make up for the missed session

25. What are associated with excessive amounts of abdominal fat?

    a. hypertension, type I diabetes, hyperlipidemia, and CAD

    b. hypertension, type I diabetes, hypolipidemia, and CAD

    c. hypotension, type II diabetes, hypolipidemia, and CAD

    d. hypertension, type II diabetes, hyperlipidemia, and CAD

26. Select the statement that best describes Mr. Vern's cholesterol and lipoprotein profile based on the following data: 34 years of age; TC 210 mg/dl; LDL-C 130 mg/dl; HDL-C 34 mg/dl; serum triglycerides 300 mg/dl.

    a. TC, LDL-C, HDL-C, and serum triglycerides are all borderline high.

    b. TC, HDL-C, and serum triglycerides are all borderline high, while LDL-C is within the desired range.

    c. TC and serum triglycerides are borderline high, while LDL-C and HDL-C are within a desirable range.

    d. TC, LDL-C, and serum triglycerides are all borderline high, while HDL-C is too low.

27. Which first-aid procedure is *not* recommended for a fracture?

    a. rest

    b. ice

    c. immobilization

    d. traction

    e. elevation

28. Besides the low back, what other area of muscle is associated with a lack of flexibility in chronic low-back pain?

    a. anterior thigh

    b. posterior thigh

    c. tibialis anterior

    d. soleus

29. Which of the following conclusions from research studies support(s) the notion that exercise is prescribed as an important component in weight management?

    a. The cumulative effects of exercise on energy expenditure can be significant.

b. Exercise and its effects may repress the appetite.

c. Exercise may minimize the loss of lean body mass.

d. *a* and *b*

e. *a*, *b*, and *c*

30. As an exercise leader, which of the following organizational patterns would allow you to systemically observe clients during an exercise session without requiring excessive movement on your part?

a. positioning yourself at one end of the gym

b. positioning yourself at one station and rotating clients through all stations

c. positioning yourself behind a one-way mirror

d. walking slowly around the perimeter of the gym

31. Which of the following muscles contribute(s) to knee extension?

a. quadriceps femoris

b. rectus femoris, vastus lateralis, vastus medialis, vastus intermedius

c. hamstring muscles and sartorius

d. *a* and *b*

e. *a*, *b*, and *c*

32. What is the end product of glycolysis that results during non-aerobic exercise?

a. pyruvate

b. lactate

c. lactate dehydrogenase

d. phosphoenolpyruvate

33. How do exercise and relaxation training compare for managing stress?

a. Relaxation training is more effective than exercise.

b. Exercise training is more effective than relaxation training.

c. Exercise and relaxation training are equally effective.

d. A combination of exercise and relaxation training is most effective.

34. What is the smallest BMI that is associated with obesity-related health risks?
    a. 20-24.9 kg/m^2
    b. 25-29.9 kg/m^2
    c. 30-40 kg/m^2
    d. > 40 kg/m^2

35. A client complains of shoulder and arm pain at rest and especially during exercise. This discomfort has developed gradually over the past two years. The client believes the pain is a simple muscle strain from shoveling snow. What should you do based on your client's complaint?
    a. Allow the client to continue aerobic activity (running), but discourage the use of resistance training until the pain has subsided.
    b. Allow the client to continue aerobic activity (jogging) and lower-body resistance training, but discontinue upper-body resistance training until the pain has subsided.
    c. Instruct the client to perform 10 extra minutes of shoulder and arm flexibility exercise before engaging in an established exercise routine.
    d. Require the client to receive physician clearance before engaging in physical activity.

36. What is the risk of death during or immediately after exercise?
    a. one death in 10 events
    b. less than one death in 100 events
    c. one death in 100 events
    d. four deaths in 500 events

37. Which of the following flexibility exercises is (are) designed to stretch the gastrocnemius, hamstrings, and spinal erectors?
    a. modified hurdler's stretch
    b. sitting toe touch
    c. side bend
    d. *a* and *b*
    e. *b* and *c*

38. Which of the following is (are) true regarding spot reducing?

   a. It uses isolated exercises in an attempt to deplete local fat deposits in a specific site.

   b. It is not effective.

   c. It has been demonstrated to be effective for abdominal fat deposits only.

   d. *a* and *b*

   e. *a, b,* and *c*

39. The exercise leader should be aware of leadership techniques that meet the needs of special populations. Which of the following pertains to the needs of young children?

   a. frequent use of demonstrations and rest periods

   b. occasional use of rest periods, frequent change in activity

   c. an occasional change in activity, use of demonstrations

   d. frequent use of demonstrations, occasional change in activity

40. Which muscles are located in the posterior thigh?

   a. the hamstring muscles

   b. the biceps femoris, semimembranosus, and semitendinosus

   c. the rectus femoris, vastus lateralis, and vastus medialis

   d. *a* and *b*

   e. *a, b,* and *c*

41. Which one of the following activities comes the closest to an energy expenditure of 10 METs?

   a. archery

   b. badminton

   c. cricket

   d. golf with motorized golf cart

   e. running a 10-minute mile

42. DOMS is most likely due to which of the following mechanisms?

   a. lactate accumulation in the muscle

   b. microscopic tears in the muscle fibers

    c. muscle spasms

    d. *a* and *b*

    e. *a*, *b*, and *c*

43. Of the following tests of flexibility, which would require the use of a goniometer?

    a. sit-and-reach

    b. modified sit-and-reach

    c. back extension

    d. straight leg raise

44. The atherosclerotic process is initiated when injury to the arterial wall is sustained in which tissue layer?

    a. adventitia

    b. endothelium

    c. intima

    d. lamina

    e. media

45. To ensure that the environment is safe, appropriate temperature, humidity, and air-circulation levels should be operating within a range of acceptable values. Of the fitness areas listed, which is (are) are in compliance with established standards?

    a. fitness testing area: temperature = 68 degrees Fahrenheit; humidity = 50 percent; air circulation = 7 exchanges per hour

    b. fitness floor: temperature = 72 degrees Fahrenheit; humidity = 60 percent; air circulation = 8 exchanges per hour

    c. gymnasium: temperature = 68 degrees Fahrenheit; humidity = 65 percent; air circulation = 15 exchanges per hour

    d. *a* and *b*

    e. *a*, *b*, and *c*

46. Which of the following best describes the resistance-training system known as "split routines"?

    a. performing three different exercises for the same body part with little to no rest between sets

b. training the legs, arms, and abdominals on Monday, Wednesday, and Friday; training the chest, shoulders, and back on Tuesday, Thursday, and Saturday

c. performing 12 repetitions of biceps curls followed immediately by 12 repetitions of triceps extension

d. performing multiple sets, starting at about 10-12 repetitions and systematically increasing resistance over several sets until only 1 repetition is possible

e. splitting exercises between upper body and lower body–for example, biceps curls followed by leg press

47. Of the vitamins listed, which water-soluble vitamin is correctly matched with its function?

a. B_1–thiamine; a coenzyme of energy metabolism

b. B_6–riboflavin; facilitates mechanism in energy metabolism

c. folic acid–B complex; a coenzyme in nucleic acids and protein synthesis

d. biotin–B complex; a coenzyme in CHO and fat metabolism

48. In which individuals is there the greatest need to periodically assess changes in physical fitness status?

a. individuals whose initial level of fitness was high and who have had a change in medication

b. individuals whose initial fitness level was low and who have had a change in medication

c. individuals who have had a change in medication and wish to change mode of activity

d. individuals whose initial fitness level was high and who wish to change mode of activity

49. Which of the following is true regarding the wearing of light (< 0.45 kilograms) ankle weights during walking or running exercise?

a. It will not alter lower-extremity ROM.

b. It appreciably alters lower-extremity ROM.

c. It increases the risk of injury to the ankle joint.

d. It is not contraindicated for individuals with orthopedic problems.

50. What is the primary energy source for performing short-term, high-intensity activity?

    a. anaerobic sources

    b. the ATP-PC system when the activity is a 400-meter dash (lasting 45 seconds)

    c. anaerobic glycolysis when the activity is a football play

    d. *a* and *b*

    e. *a, b,* and *c*

51. What should the exercise professional use to palpate the radial pulse?

    a. the thumb

    b. the thumb and first finger

    c. the first two fingers

    d. a stethoscope

52. What class of medication causes a decrease in both resting and exercise HR?

    a. ACE inhibitors

    b. bronchodilators

    c. beta blockers

    d. diuretics

53. Some clients requesting admission into an exercise facility may refuse to obtain medical clearance as warranted by a screening process prior to exercise participation. How should this situation be handled?

    a. The participant should be told to procure medical clearance or there will be no admission.

    b. The participant will be required to sign an "assumption of risk" document if one is recognized by the local jurisdiction.

    c. A medical clearance is not required if the individual has fewer than two risks for heart disease and is under the age of 25 years.

    d. *a* and *b*

    e. *a, b,* and *c*

54. Which of the following could be used as a basis for evaluating the effectiveness of a group exercise program?

    a. the number of participants who invited friends to join the exercise group

    b. the percentage of hypertensive individuals who now have their BP under control

    c. the number of participants who attended all exercise sessions

    d. *a, b,* and *c*

55. Thirst lags behind the body's need for water. Which of the following is (are) used to prevent dehydration?

    a. drinking one cup of water every 15 minutes during exercise

    b. consuming 200-400 milliliters of water every 20 minutes during exercise

    c. consuming 500 milliliters of water every 30 minutes during exercise

    d. *a* and *b*

    e. *a, b,* and *c*

56. Program costs can vary from less than $50.00 to more than $600.00 per employee. As part of the Health/Fitness Instructor's responsibilities, program costs must be well maintained within the facility's budgetary guidelines. Below are listed types of facilities and approximate costs for exercise program resources. Of the following, which is feasible?

    a. community-based program–walk, jog, cycle exercise routes; $100.00 per month per employee

    b. YMCA–exercise testing, exercise prescription, exercise classes; $200.00 per month per employee

    c. university fitness program–fitness testing, exercise prescription, exercise classes; $50.00 per month per employee

    d. self-help exercise program–social service organization; $40.00 per month per employee

57. Movements of elevation, depression, abduction, adduction, upward rotation, and downward rotation can all be found in which joint?

   a. hip
   b. shoulder
   c. wrist
   d. ankle

58. Exercise activities lasting longer than 45 seconds use which of the following energy systems to provide ATP?

   a. ATP-PC system
   b. anaerobic glycolysis
   c. oxidative phosphorylation
   d. *a* and *b*
   e. *a*, *b*, and *c*

59. Of the five Korotkoff sounds (phases), which is considered to represent DBP in adults?

   a. 1
   b. 2
   c. 3
   d. 4
   e. 5

60. A 45-year-old, apparently healthy male was lifting weights in a recreation-center facility. He noted that for the last 15 minutes of his workout, there was a persistent pain in his shoulder and arm. Breathing rate increased, but did not seem out of the ordinary because of the heavy exercises he was performing. His skin was moist and pale. What would initial first-aid management for this situation include?

   a. stopping the participant from all exercise and requiring him to rest
   b. placing the participant in a sitting position to make it easier for him to breathe
   c. questioning the participant about possible heart disease and medications

    d. *a* and *b*

    e. *a, b,* and *c*

61. Which of the following best describes the ACSM exercise prescription guideline for improving muscular strength/endurance?

    a. three sets of 8-10 exercises designed to train the major muscle groups, performed at least four days per week, using 8-12 repetitions per set

    b. one set of 8-10 exercises designed to train the major muscle groups, performed at least two days per week, using 4-8 repetitions per set

    c. three sets of 8-10 exercises designed to train the major muscle groups, performed at least three days per week, using 8-12 repetitions per set

    d. one set of 8-10 exercises designed to train the major muscle groups, performed at least two days per week, using 8-12 repetitions per set

62. In 1977, in response to the health problems observed in Americans, a U.S. Senate Select Committee on Nutrition and Human Needs formulated the "U.S. Dietary Goals." Which of the statements listed is from that document?

    a. Reduce cholesterol to 500 milligrams/day.

    b. Decrease saturated fat to represent 30 percent of the total caloric intake.

    c. Increase CHO intake to represent 55-60 percent of the total caloric content.

    d. Substitute nonfat milk for whole milk and potassium-chloride salt for sodium-chloride salt.

63. A system of record keeping is essential to the operation of a successful organization. A filing system should be created that is efficient and cost effective. Which of the following ideas would be of value with regard to the way a facility is keeping its records?

    a. All information concerning a client and his/her account should be kept on three separate cards with the following information: card 1–personal information; card 2–membership information; card 3–account information

   b. Information about a client's exercise performance, etc., for a day should be recorded and filed on that day.

   c. It is more efficient and cost effective to allow similar types of records about individual clients to accumulate and then file all similar reports at one time, preferably on a weekly basis.

   d. All files and records should be examined weekly for errors, and superfluous materials in the client's file should be removed.

64. The amount of movement within a specific joint (ROM) is limited by which of the following?

   a. the bony structures of two articulating surfaces

   b. the length of the ligaments

   c. the length of the bone

   d. *a* and *b*

   e. *a, b,* and *c*

65. Isometric exercise may present hazards to the participant. Which of the following might be viewed as more of a risk with isometric as compared to isotonic exercise?

   a. increase in left ventricular wall pressure loading; increase in DBP

   b. increase in HR; increase in SBP

   c. increase in left ventricular wall pressure loading; increase in rate-pressure product; increase in SBP

   d. increase in left ventricular wall volume loading; increase in SBP; increase in DBP

66. For which of the following individuals would medical clearance be warranted before the administration of an exercise test?

   a. a 25-year-old male with one CAD risk factor (no signs or symptoms) who wishes to perform vigorous exercise

   b. a 25-year-old female with two CAD risk factors (no signs or symptoms) who wishes to perform vigorous exercise

   c. a 33-year-old female, diagnosed two years ago with non-insulin-dependent diabetes with no additional CAD risk factors (no signs or symptoms), who wishes to perform vigorous exercise

    d. *a* and *c*

    e. *b* and *c*

67. During lunch, a 21-year-old diabetic male decided to play pick-up basketball in the company recreational facility. After about 30 minutes of exercise, he began to experience dizziness, confusion, and fatigue and was told that he looked ill. He was still conscious. What initial first aid should you perform?

    a. Give him some oral glucose or sugar water.

    b. You suspect hyperglycemia, so help the young man give himself an insulin shot.

    c. You suspect hyperglycemia, which rules out giving any oral sugar or glucose; call the EMS.

    d. Rush the young man to the hospital before he enters into a diabetic coma.

68. What do ACSM exercise prescription guidelines suggest for improving flexibility?

    a. stretching at least two days per week, holding each stretch for 75-90 seconds and performing three to five repetitions for each dynamic stretch

    b. stretching at least two days per week, holding each stretch for 60-90 seconds and performing one to two repetitions for each static stretch

    c. stretching at least three days per week, holding each stretch for 45-60 seconds and performing one to two repetitions for each dynamic stretch

    d. stretching at least three days per week, holding each stretch for 10-30 seconds and performing three to five repetitions for each static stretch

69. Which devices and purported benefits for weight-loss programs is (are) correctly matched?

    a. rubber suit–fat reduction

    b. vibrating belt–break-up of fat, which will lead to weight loss

    c. sauna–weight loss

    d. *a* and *b*

    e. *a, b,* and *c*

70. A variety of educational programs and materials can be used to help clients enhance their health and fitness status. Listed below are educational approaches followed by materials that could be used in the approach. Which pairs are correct?

    a. large group–audiovisuals, newsletters, brochures
    b. small group–self-instruction kits, audiovisuals, games
    c. individual–programmed instruction, interactive computer learning, self-instruction kit
    d. *a* and *b*
    e. *a, b,* and *c*

71. Which of the following is (are) a common foot strike pattern(s) in running?

    a. striking the ground with rear foot–subtalar joint in supination–pronation
    b. striking the ground at midfoot–slight backward motion–toe-off
    c. striking the ground on toe–falling back on heel–rolling foot lateral to medial
    d. *a* and *b*
    e. *a, b,* and *c*

72. Typically, within three weeks of detraining, which of the following changes in physiological function are likely to occur?

    a. decrease in cardiovascular conditioning; decrease in SV max; decrease in $\dot{V}O_2$max
    b. decrease in plasma volume; decrease in SV max; decrease in mitochondrial enzyme level to a pretraining state
    c. increase in $\dot{V}O_2$ at submaximal workloads; increase in ventilation at submaximal workloads; increase in HR at submaximal levels
    d. *a* and *b*
    e. *a, b,* and *c*

73. Which statement is composed of only relative contraindications to exercise testing?

    a. resting DBP > 115 mm Hg; ventricular aneurysm; third-degree AV block without pacemaker

b. fixed-rate pacemaker; mononucleosis; advanced pregnancy

c. chronic infectious disease; acute infection; moderate valvu-
    lar heart disease

d. unstable angina; thrombophlebitis; significant emotional
    distress

74. To adhere to the principle of specificity, which exercise should
     be employed by a volleyball player who wants to improve
     vertical-jump ability?

a. barbell squats

b. seated knee extensions

c. seated leg press

d. seated knee flexion

75. Which of the following identifies the actual number of kilo-
     calories in one gram of nutrient?

a. fat–9.45 kcal/g; CHO–4.3 kcal/g; protein–5.65 kcal/g;
    alcohol–7.0 kcal/g

b. fat–8.0 kcal/g; CHO–3.0 kcal/g; protein–4.0 kcal/g;
    alcohol–7.0 kcal/g

c. fat–7.0 kcal/g; CHO–5.0 kcal/g; protein–5.0 kcal/g;
    alcohol–7.2 kcal/g

d. *a* and *b*

e. *a, b,* and *c*

76. What procedure should the fitness professional follow when
     administering the Cooper 12-minute test of aerobic capacity?

a. Instruct the participant to run, not walk, for the entire test.

b. Instruct the participant to walk, not run, for the entire test.

c. Mark the track by placing marker cones every 40-55 yards.

d. Tell the participant that the test is completed when 1 mile has
    been covered.

e. *a, b,* and *c*

77. To what is the striated appearance of a skeletal muscle fiber due?

a. myofibril arrangements

b. actin and myosin protein filaments

c. overlap of the I band and H zone

d. *a* and *b*

e. *a, b,* and *c*

78. When an exercise participant is being positioned on a cycle ergometer, the seat should be adjusted to a height that would allow the knee joint to be in what position when the pedal is at the bottom of the downstroke?

a. straight

b. flexed, approximately 5 degrees

c. flexed, approximately 10 degrees

d. extended, approximately 5 degrees

e. extended, approximately 10 degrees

79. Exercise involving the lactic acid source of energy production generally incorporates what exercise-to-rest ratio?

a. 1:1

b. 1:2

c. 1:3

d. 1:4

e. 1:5

80. Weekly weight-loss goals for medically unsupervised weight-loss programs include which of the following?

a. 2 pounds/week

b. 1,000 kcal dietary deficit per week

c. 7,000 kcal total per week

d. *a* and *b*

e. *a, b,* and *c*

81. Which of the following is (are) true regarding the training of staff?

a. It is needed in order to orient a new employee to the organization's philosophy, programs, staff, and participants.

b. It can include attendance at professional conferences and continuing education classes.

    c. It involves continuing development in communication.

    d. *a* and *b*

    e. *a, b,* and *c*

82. The events of the excitation-coupling and contraction phases of the sliding filament theory are listed randomly below. What is the correct order?

    a. Muscle fiber is stimulated; action potential travels through the T tubule; Ca^{++} is released from the sarcoplasmic reticulum; Ca^{++} saturates troponin, turning on actin; ATP on the cross-bridge is charged; actomyosin is formed; ATP → ADP + Pi + ENERGY; energy release swivels the cross-bridge; actin slides over myosin.

    b. Muscle fiber is stimulated; Ca^{++} is released from the sarcoplasmic reticulum; action potential travels through the T tubule; Ca^{++} saturates troponin, turning on actin; ATP on the cross-bridge is charged; actomyosin is formed; energy release swivels the cross-bridge; actin slides over myosin; ATP → ADP + Pi + ENERGY.

    c. ATP on the cross-bridge is charged; ATP → ADP + Pi + ENERGY; action potential travels through the T tubule; muscle fiber is stimulated; Ca^{++} is released from the sarcoplasmic reticulum; Ca^{++} saturates troponin, turning on actin; actomyosin is formed; energy release swivels the cross-bridge; actin slides over myosin.

    d. Muscle fiber is stimulated; action potential travels through the T tubule; Ca^{++} saturates troponin, turning on actin; Ca^{++} is released from the sarcoplasmic reticulum; ATP on the cross-bridge is charged; actomyosin is formed; ATP → ADP + Pi + ENERGY; energy release swivels the cross-bridge; actin slides over myosin.

83. Which procedure is best when testing children on a treadmill?

    a. adjusting grade and speed simultaneously

    b. adjusting grade only and leaving speed constant

    c. adjusting speed only and leaving grade constant

    d. administering a cycle ergometer test, since treadmill testing with children is not appropriate

84. What most affects evaporative heat loss during exercise?
    a. ambient temperature
    b. air-current speed
    c. percentage of skin surface exposed to the environment
    d. relative humidity

85. Which of the following is (are) true regarding dietary fats?
    a. They serve as an energy source.
    b. They provide an insulating layer to inhibit heat loss beneath the skin.
    c. They serve as a vehicle for fat-soluble vitamin utilization.
    d. *a* and *b*
    e. *a, b,* and *c*

86. How can the strength of contraction in a muscle be graded?
    a. multiple motor unit summation
    b. wave summation
    c. varying the frequency of contraction of individual motor units
    d. *a* and *b*
    e. *a, b,* and *c*

87. Which of the following BP responses would represent a general indication to discontinue a GXT in an apparently healthy adult?
    a. 15 mm Hg drop in SBP with an increase in exercise intensity
    b. rise in SBP to 240 mm Hg
    c. failure of DBP to increase with an increase in exercise intensity
    d. *a* and *c*

88. What is (are) the recommendation(s) for the current U.S. diet for distribution of calories from CHO?
    a. 58 percent of daily calories
    b. 48 percent from complex CHOs and 10 percent from simple sugars
    c. 75 percent from all sources
    d. *a* and *b*
    e. *a, b,* and *c*

89. Which of the following abnormal conditions is matched cor-
    rectly with the appropriate normal symptom?
    a. hypoxia–cessation of breathing
    b. hypoventilation–12-15 breaths per minute
    c. orthostatic hypotension–120/80 mm Hg in a horizontal
       position
    d. dyspnea–labored breathing

90. What is the recommended intake of protein for an adult male or
    female?
    a. 10 percent of total calories; 0.8 g/kg body weight
    b. 10 percent of total calories; 0.9 g/kg body weight
    c. 12 percent of total calories; 0.8 g/kg body weight
    d. 12 percent of total calories; 0.9 g/kg body weight

91. Compared to leg work, arm work demonstrates what types of
    SBP and DBP values?
    a. higher systolic values, lower diastolic values
    b. no differences in systolic values, no differences in diastolic
       values
    c. high systolic values, higher diastolic values
    d. higher systolic values; no differences in diastolic values

92. What measure of regional fat distribution is associated with an
    increased risk of CAD in men and women?
    a. waist:hip ratio
    b. abdominal:gluteal ratio
    c. android:gynoid ratio
    d. *a* and *b*
    e. *a, b,* and *c*

93. The risk of disease increases when the waist-to-hip ratio exceeds
    what value in men and women, respectively?
    a. $> 0.7; > 0.6$
    b. $> 0.8; > 0.7$
    c. $> 0.9; > 0.8$
    d. $> 1.00; > 0.9$

94. Given the following information, what is the energy cost for a bench-stepping exercise? step height = 20 centimeters; step rate = 20 steps per minute; weight of subject = 55 kilograms

   a. 4.7 METs; 4.8 kcal/kg/hr

   b. 4.8 METs; 16.73 ml/kg/min

   c. 4.7 METs; 4.6 kcal/min

   d. 5.8 METs; 4.8 kcal/min

95. Given the following information, what is the energy cost for leg cycle ergometry exercise? work rate = 600 kgm/min (100 watts); weight of subject = 50 kilograms

   a. 7.86 METs; 6.87 kcal/min

   b. 8.6 METs; 7.5 kcal/min

   c. 8.86 METs; 27.50 ml/kg/min

   d. 8.6 METs; 8.7 kcal/kg/hr

96. What is the energy cost for a 170-pound, 21-year-old male walking on a treadmill at 90 m/min up a 12% grade?

   a. 3.6 METs; 3.1 kcal/min

   b. 3.6 METs; 3.6 kcal/kg/hr

   c. 9.12 METs; 8.0 kcal/kg/hr

   d. 9.12 METs; 12.34 kcal/min

97. What is the energy cost for a 125-pound, 35-year-old female running at 90 m/min up a 10% grade on a treadmill?

56.8 Kg

   a. 8.46 METs; 8.40 kcal/min

   b. 9.1 METs; 7.2 kcal/min

   c. 8.46 METs; 22.03 ml/kg/min

   d. 9.1 METs; 7.4 kcal/kg/hr

98. Given the following information, what is the energy cost of horizontal running? distance = 10 kilometers; time = 60 minutes; weight of subject = 50 kilograms

   a. 10.5 METs; 9.2 kcal/min

   b. 11.52 METs; 11.1 kcal/kg/hr

   c. 10.5 METs; 10.7 kcal/kg/hr

   d. 10.14 METs; 9.2 kcal/min

99. Given the following information, what is the energy cost of graded running? speed = 100 m/min; grade = 10%; weight of subject = 50 kilograms

   a. 9.2 METs; 17.94 ml/kg/min

   b. 9.2 METs; 8.1 kcal/min

   c. 9.2 METs; 10.4 kcal/kg/hr

   d. *a* and *b*

   e. *a, b,* and *c*

100. A 45-year-old, 125-pound female exercised on an arm cycle ergometer at 600 kgm/min. What was her energy cost for this activity?

   a. 7.35 METs; 7.35 kcal/min

   b. 35.18 ml/kg/min

   c. 7.35 kcal/kg/hr

   d. *a* and *b*

   e. *a, b,* and *c*

101. A 200-pound male exercised on a bicycle ergometer for 20 minutes at 2 kiloponds. What was his energy cost?

   a. 25452 milliliters O_2

   b. 127.3 kcal

   c. 4.2 kcal/kg/hr

   d. *a* and *b*

   e. *a, b,* and *c*

102. What is the energy cost for a 156-pound male, age 23 years, running on a level treadmill at 6 mph?

   a. 10.19 METs

   b. 35.68 ml/kg/min

   c. 12.65 kcal/min

   d. *a* and *b*

   e. *a, b,* and *c*

103. A 125-pound female pedals a Monark cycle ergometer at 50 rev/min against a resistance of 3.0 kilograms. What is the power output? What is her relative $\dot{V}O_2$?

　　a.　900 kgm/m; 35.2 ml/kg/min

　　b.　900 kgm/m; 227.5 ml O_2/min

　　c.　600 kgm/m; 1998.5 ml/kg/min

　　d.　600 kgm/m; 1998.5 milliliters

Practice Examination Blank Score Sheet

Appendix B contains a blank score sheet for the practice examination. For each question there is a blank space where you can write the answer to each question and another blank space where you can write the correct answer to questions you have missed. This will make it much easier for you to review those questions on which you were incorrect. Also included is a column in which to enter the KSA that each answer corresponds with. Note that this blank score sheet does not mirror the score sheet used during the actual exam. For the actual exam you will be asked to use a scan sheet.

Question #	Your Answer	Correct Answer	KSA # Category
1	A		
2	A		
3	B		
4	B		
5	B		
6	C		
7	E		
8	D		
9	C		

Question #	Your Answer	Correct Answer	KSA # Category
✗ 10	D	E	Program Adm & Mangm
11	A		
12	C		
13	C		
14	B		
15	E		
✗ 16	D	C	Patho & R.F.
17	C		
18	B		
19	A		
20	A		
✗ 21	E	D	Anatomy & Bio Mechan
22	A		
✗ 23	A	D	Development & Aging
24	B		
25	D		
26	D		
✗ 27	B	D	Emergency Procedures & Saf
28	B		
29	E		
30	B		
✗ 31	B	D	Anatomy + Biomechanics
32	B		
33	D		

Question #	Your Answer	Correct Answer	KSA # Category
34	B		
35	D		
36	B		
37	D		
X 38	B	D	Nutrition & Wt. Mange
39	A		
40	D		
41	E		
X 42	E	B	Ex Phys
43	D		
44	B		
X 45	E	D	Emergency Procedure
46	B		
X 47	D	B	Nutrition
48	B		
X 49	C	A	Anatomy + Bio Mech
X 50	E	A	Exercise Procedures
51	C		
52	C		
X 53	A	B	Emergency Procedure
X 54	D	B	Exercise Programming
55	E		
56	C		
X 57	A	B	Anatomy & Biomechanics

Question #	Your Answer	Correct Answer	KSA # Category
✗ 58	D	E	EX. Phys
59	E		
60	E		
61	D		
62	C		
✗ 63	C	B	Program Adm & Mngmen
64	D		
✗ 65	B	A	Ex. Phys
✗ 66	B	D	Health Appraisal
✗ 67	B	A	Emergency Proced.
68	D		
69	E		
70	E		
71	D		
✗ 72	D	A	Ex. Phys
✗ 73	C	B	Health Appr.
74	A		
75	A		
76	C		
77	D		
78	B		
✗ 79	C	B	EX. Programing
80	E		
81	E		

Question #	Your Answer	Correct Answer	KSA # Category
82	B	A	Ex. Phys
83	C	B	Appraisal + Testing
84	C	D	Ex. Programming
85	E		
86	D	E	Ex. Phys
87	A		
88	D		
89	C	B	Ex. Phys
90	C		
91	B	C	Ex. Phys
92	A	E	Nutrition
93	B	C	Nutrition
94			
95			
96			
97			
98			
99			
100			
101			
102			
103			

APPENDIX C

Answers to the Practice Examination

SEQUENTIAL LIST OF ANSWERS

1. a	2. a	3. b
4. b	5. b	6. c
7. e	8. d	9. c
10. e	11. a	12. c
13. c	14. b	15. e
16. c	17. c	18. b
19. a	20. a	21. d
22. a	23. d	24. b
25. d	26. d	27. d
28. b	29. e	30. b
31. d	32. b	33. d
34. b	35. d	36. b
37. d	38. d	39. a
40. d	41. e	42. b

43. d	44. b	45. d
46. b	47. b	48. b
49. a	50. a	51. c
52. c	53. b	54. b
55. e	56. c	57. b
58. e	59. e	60. e
61. d	62. c	63. b
64. d	65. a	66. d
67. a	68. d	69. e
70. e	71. d	72. a
73. b	74. a	75. a
76. c	77. d	78. b
79. b	80. e	81. e
82. a	83. b	84. d
85. e	86. e	87. a
88. d	89. b	90. c
91. c	92. e	93. c
94. b	95. a	96. d
97. a	98. b	99. b
100. b	101. e	102. e
103. a		

ANSWERS TO THE PRACTICE EXAMINATION BY KSA CATEGORY

In this section we have listed the answers to the practice questions according to KSA category. After taking and grading your practice examination, you can mark the questions that you did not answer correctly and write in the corresponding KSA. This will help give you an accurate picture of your weak and strong areas.

FUNCTIONAL ANATOMY AND BIOMECHANICS

1. a	11. a	21. d
31. d	40. d	49. a
57. b	64. d	71. d

EXERCISE PHYSIOLOGY

2. a	12. c	22. a
32. b	41. e	42. b
50. a	58. e	65. a
72. a	77. d	82. d
86. e	89. b	91. c

HUMAN DEVELOPMENT AND AGING

3. b	13. c	23. d

PATHOPHYSIOLOGY AND RISK FACTORS

6. c	16. c	26. d
35. d	44. b	52. c

HUMAN BEHAVIOR AND PSYCHOLOGY

4. b	14. b	24. b
33. d		

HEALTH APPRAISAL AND FITNESS TESTING

5. b	15. e	25. d
34. b	43. d	51. c
59. e	66. d	73. b
78. b	83. b	87. a

EMERGENCY PROCEDURES AND SAFETY

7. e	17. c	27. d
36. b	45. d	53. b
60. e	67. a	

EXERCISE PROGRAMMING

8. d	18. b	28. b
37. d	46. b	54. b
61. d	68. d	74. a
79. b	84. d	

NUTRITION AND WEIGHT MANAGEMENT

9. c	19. a	29. e
38. d	47. b	55. e
62. c	69. e	75. a
80. e	85. e	88. d
90. c	92. e	93. c

PROGRAM ADMINISTRATION AND MANAGEMENT

10. e	20. a	30. b
39. a	48. b	56. c
63. b	70. e	76. c
81. e		

METABOLIC EQUATIONS

94. b	95. a	96. d
97. a	98. b	99. e
100. e	101. e	102. e
103. a		

APPENDIX D

Practice Exam Profile Sheet

Use this profile sheet to determine the percentage of questions you answered correctly for each KSA category and for the entire practice exam. Use the following steps to determine your score.

Step One: After finishing the practice exam, use appendix C to score your exam. Mark all incorrect responses by placing the correct answer in the space provided.

Step Two: For each incorrect response, note its corresponding KSA category by placing a tally mark in the appropriate KSA category tally column on the profile sheet. Subtract your tally from the maximum score for the KSA to derive your score. Divide your score by the maximum score to derive the percentage of correct responses for each KSA category. We suggest marking any KSA category below 75% as an area needing further study.

Step Three: To calculate your overall test score, simply total the column labeled "Your Score" and divide this sum by the total number of test questions—103. Remember, in order to receive certification, you will need to score about 70% (according to current standards).

KSA Category	Tally	Maximum Score	Your Score	Percent Correct	Check Categories in Need of Improvement
Functional Anatomy and Biomechanics	4x	9	5	55%	✓
Exercise Physiology	9x	15	6	40%	✓
Human Development and Aging	1x	3	2	66%	✓
Pathophysiology / Risk Factors	1x	6	5	83%	
Human Behavior / Psychology	0	4	4	100%	
Health Appraisal and Fitness Testing	3x	12	9	75%	
Emergency Procedures and Safety	4x	8	4	50%	✓
Exercise Programming	3x	11	8	73%	
Nutrition and Weight Management	4x	15	11	73%	
Program Administration / Management	2x	10	8	80%	
Metabolic Equations		10			
Totals		103			

ABOUT THE AUTHORS

Larry Isaacs is a professor of exercise science at Wright State University in Dayton, Ohio. He has worked at the university since 1979, teaching both undergraduate and graduate students in courses covering exercise prescription, motor development, motor learning, and research methods. He is responsible for developing the school's exercise science/pre-physical therapy program within the Department of Biological Sciences.

Isaacs received his PhD from the University of Maryland in 1979. His areas of concentration included motor development, physiological growth and development, research and statistics, and administration. A prolific writer, Isaacs is the author or coauthor of 10 other books and numerous scholarly articles. He is a Research Fellow of the American Alliance for Health, Physical Education, Recreation and Dance, and he is a member of the American College of Sports Medicine, with whom he is certified as a Health/Fitness Instructor.

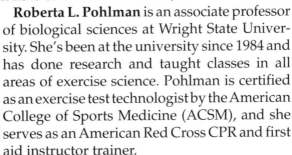

Roberta L. Pohlman is an associate professor of biological sciences at Wright State University. She's been at the university since 1984 and has done research and taught classes in all areas of exercise science. Pohlman is certified as an exercise test technologist by the American College of Sports Medicine (ACSM), and she serves as an American Red Cross CPR and first aid instructor trainer.

After receiving her PhD in exercise physiology from The Ohio State University in 1982, Pohlman went on to complete a two-year postdoctoral fellowship in research at St. Louis University Medical School. She is a coauthor of one other book. She also has served on the editorial advisory committee for *Future Focus*—a journal of the Ohio Association for Health, Physical Education and Recreation—and on the editorial review boards for *Strategies* and *JOHPERD*, which are both journals of the American Alliance for Health, Physical Education, Recreation and Dance. Pohlman is a member of ACSM and the American Physiological Society.